BRUNETTE

AMBITION

BRUNETTE AMBITION

LEA MICHELE

CROWN ARCHETYPE
NEW YORK

Published in the United States by
CROWN ARCHETYPE,
an imprint of the Crown Publishing Group,
a division of Random House LLC,
a Penguin Random House Company,
New York.
www.crownpublishing.com

Crown Archetype with colophon is a trademark of
RANDOM HOUSE LLC.

Library of Congress Cataloging-in-Publication Data
Michele, Lea.
Brunette ambition/Lea Michele.
    p.   cm.
1. Self-help–Personal Growth–General. 2. Biography &
Autobiography–Entertainment & Performing Arts. 3. Self-help.
BF697.S46
2013050624

ISBN 978-0-8041-3907-6
eBook ISBN 978-0-8041-3908-3

Printed in the United States of America

Book design by JENNIFER K. BEAL DAVIS for BALLAST DESIGN
Photography credits: see page 207
Jacket design by Michael Nagin
Jacket photography: Peggy Sirota (front cover); Justin Coit (back
cover: fashion, food, fitness); Lea Michele (back cover: cat)

10 9 8 7 6 5 4 3 2 1
FIRST EDITION

This book is dedicated to my
beautiful mother:
Thank you for being the safety
net that has always allowed me
to reach for the stars.

LETTER TO FANS 9

CHAPTER 1: WHAT MAKES ME ME 11

CHAPTER 2: THE BIZ 27

CHAPTER 3: SELF-CARE 101 47

CHAPTER 4: FOR THE LOVE OF FOOD 63

CHAPTER 5: LIVING THE FIT LIFE 91

CHAPTER 6: EVERYDAY STYLE 109

CHAPTER 7: RED CARPET FASHION 121

CHAPTER 8: HOLLYWOOD GLAM 135

CHAPTER 9: FRIENDSHIP 169

CHAPTER 10: MY LIFE WITH *GLEE* 187

UNTIL NEXT TIME 203

ACKNOWLEDGMENTS 205

ENTS

TO THE
GREATEST
FANS ON
EARTH

've been so lucky in my life—in *Glee* and beyond—to have such an incredible support system in all of you. You've really made this journey so wonderful, and I most certainly wouldn't be where I am today without you.

This book is the story of how I got to where I am today—as incredible and unexpected as that journey has been. My hope is that you take something from it that will inspire and motivate you, and also make you realize that anything you want to accomplish in your life is completely possible. After all—through some remarkable luck and a lot of hard work—I've managed to make many of my dreams come true.

I especially want to thank my biggest fan, Cory, who read almost every chapter of this book. He, too, was so thankful for all the support I had from all of you. He very much lives on in these pages: Not only did he give me a ton of practical feedback in terms of notes and edits, but he shines through in everything that I've done in my life and has been an incredible source of love and inspiration. I

WHAT MAKES ME ME

> *"A human being is only interesting if he's in contact with himself. I learned you have to trust yourself, be what you are, and do what you ought to do the way you should do it."*
> —BARBRA STREISAND

I firmly believe that where you come from makes you *you*—and that when you celebrate your roots and focus on how those roots make you distinct, you have the greatest chance of becoming your best self. Fortunately, the world is becoming more and more attuned to uniqueness, to celebrating everything that makes us all a bit different—so ignoring those quirks that make you stand out is a mistake. I never tried to put myself in a box, or attempted to "fit in," because I really only knew how to play myself. I think this is because my parents instilled so much self-confidence in me and constantly reassured me that I was just great as I was. I'm so proud of who I am, and I owe it all to my family.

They're the essence of my being and the foundation of my story.

And my story begins in the Bronx, where I was born to a Jewish father and an Italian mother. My parents met when they were teenagers at the neighborhood playground. Picture this: My father, complete with a giant Jew fro, approached my mother on roller skates and asked her to smell his hair. Herbal Essences had just hit the shelves, and he figured it would make an excellent impression. Apparently it did, because they've been married for more than thirty years.

Though they theoretically grew up on the same block, my parents couldn't have been from more different worlds. My father is from a small, traditional Jewish family, whereas my mom is from a huge Italian clan (I have nineteen younger cousins on one side alone). My parents are more complementary than similar—but they're best friends, regardless. My mother is a retired nurse, and I get my emotional, nurturing side from her, as well as my ability to get through hard moments. She hasn't always had an easy time. Her childhood was incredibly rough: She lost three of her six siblings, for one thing. And later, it wasn't all roses either: When I was nineteen, she was diagnosed with uterine cancer. But while she has every reason to be upset about the things she's gone through, she's never played the victim. She's the most loving and caring and strong woman and is always taking care of everyone else.

I'M *ALWAYS* PUTTING MYSELF OUT THERE; I'M NEVER COMPLACENT, I'M NEVER PASSIVE; I'M ALWAYS LOOKING FOR THE NEXT OPPORTUNITY. MY DAD TAUGHT ME HOW TO HUSTLE.

Meanwhile, my father, a former deli owner, is an incredibly hard worker who is always hustling. He's also a jokester and makes everything fun. He gave me his work ethic and his ability to make something out of nothing. When I was in high school, he sold his deli and got into real estate, and vastly improved our lives: He's one of those guys who will always go after what he wants and would never think to passively stand around and wait for opportunity to knock. He will meet someone at a party and close a real estate deal twenty minutes later; when we shared a box with Slash at the Super Bowl, he pitched himself so hard as a potential backup singer for Guns N' Roses (he has no musical background but was determined that they should collaborate), I really thought Slash might make room for him in the band. Whether he's serious or kidding around, my dad lives his life without fear and has no shame about putting himself out there. His philosophy is that nobody is going to come to you, begging you to take a job (or in my case, a role). I learned to stay on my toes from him. Because of this, if you were to meet me, you'd think I didn't actually have a job. I'm *always* putting myself out there; I'm never complacent; I'm never passive; I'm always looking for the next opportunity. My dad taught me how to hustle.

When I was four, my parents decided that they didn't want me to become hardened by city life, and so we moved from the Bronx to a more pastoral stretch of New Jersey. It was there that a bizarre but wonderful twist of fate led me to be cast on Broadway (more on that later). The term *stage parents* makes my skin crawl, but my mom and dad were pretty much the opposite of the cliché. For one, it was *never* part of their plan. They would never have guessed in a million years when they had Lea Michele Sarfati on August 29, 1986, that she would work on Broadway and go on to be on a TV show in Los Angeles. They were completely unassuming about the entire thing. They were just a deli owner and a full-time nurse, whose sole ambition was to raise a happy

and healthy daughter. They didn't wear my early success as a badge, and they didn't live vicariously through me—it was my thing, and they did not step into my spotlight. My acting career was just this extracurricular activity that I did and that made me happy, and my apparent delight in it was enough of a reason for them to let me keep doing it. The fact that they never applied any pressure, and never supplied an agenda for me, is why I'm still acting and singing today. I would be nothing without my upbringing: The color and texture it has supplied is why I am who I am—and not to oversimplify things, but it's because I'm not like all the other girls that I've gotten to where I am today.

↑ Clockwise from top left: Family vacation with my mom and dad ✱ as the little girl in *Ragtime*, my second Broadway show ✱ my mom and Aunt Carmela at my baptism ✱ my dad and Slash at the Super Bowl.

FINDING ROLE MODELS

When I was growing up, nobody on the popular television shows looked like me. My favorite show was *Saved by the Bell,* and while I adored all of the kids in those high school halls, I couldn't see myself in any of them. I'm sure people would expect that would make a girl sad, but my mom made sure that I saw there was a world outside of basic cable. She was always playing old movies like *West Side Story* and *Funny Girl,* which is how I came to discover women like Natalie Wood and Barbra Streisand. (In fact, my parents used to tell me that I seemed like I could be the love child of Jim Carrey and Natalie Wood.) Seeing those women act brought out a light inside of me and made me feel so alive: There was something about them that reminded me of myself. I was gawky and awkward like Barbra but understood that she was still considered beautiful, which I found so comforting. When I watched *Funny Girl,* it totally resonated with me that Barbra's sense of humor is the thing that makes her so attractive. And once I eventually realized I could sing, Natalie and Barbra spoke to me even more: I wanted to do what they did. I would reenact the scene in *West Side Story* when Maria stands over Tony's body constantly. While some of my friends were living in the world of *90210* with cute boys and tons of hairspray, I was living in the world of *The Wizard of Oz* with singing trees and ruby slippers. One of the things about *Glee* that's so great is that it presents a high school world that's so varied, so wonderfully odd, so multicolored and dimensional, that I know kids everywhere can see themselves reflected back. Search the world for a role model until you find someone who resonates with your soul: It's so important, and so *comforting,* to have lampposts in this world who can light the way.

THE DAY I MET BARBRA

In January 2011, Barbra Streisand was honored at the Grammys, and as is the tradition there was a MusiCares benefit on her behalf a few nights before the ceremony. I was invited to sing, since my love for Barbra is pretty well-known, which was incredibly exciting. There was a plethora of incredibly talented musicians on the roster, who were all doing renditions of her songs: Faith Hill, Stevie Wonder, Seal . . . and so I sang "My Man," from *Funny Girl*, which is my favorite song in the entire world. And there she was in the audience, right in front of me. I was incredibly nervous—there was nothing that could have fully prepared me to sing in front of my idol—but I was so honored and happy to be on that stage that I just powered through my performance.

I was hoping to meet her that night, but she was surrounded by a sea of people, and as I made my way toward her, her team whisked her away. I figured I had lost my chance forever.

I attended the Grammys a few nights later because I was presenting an award; Barbra sang four songs that night, and "Evergreen," which I love, was one of them. It was the first time I had ever heard her sing live. I left the Grammys early, in order to avoid the post-event valet rush, and was standing there in the quiet before the storm waiting for my car when I felt a tap on my shoulder. I turned around, and it was Barbra. And she said, "I just wanted to say thank you for introducing me to your generation." And I gave her a big hug and told her that I thought she was amazing, and she looked at me and asked, "Did I sound good tonight?" And I said, "You were incredible." And that was it. The minute she walked away, I started to cry hysterically. Sometimes you meet your idols and they don't live up to your expectations, but that moment was one of the best in my life. As soon as my car pulled up I called Ryan Murphy to tell him that it was over: I had met Barbra and didn't need to be in this business anymore. All my dreams had come true.

This past November, Chris Colfer and I went to see her at the Hollywood Bowl with Dante Di Loreto, one of the producers from *Glee*. It was a gorgeous night to sit under the stars and listen to Barbra; she sounded so beautiful and seemed so relaxed. Chris and I held hands the entire time and cried, especially when she sang "Happy Days Are Here Again," which Chris and I sang on *Glee* together and performed during all the *Glee* concert tours. At the end of the concert Chris wanted us to go backstage to say hi, but I didn't want to mar my perfect moment of meeting Barbra at the Grammys. Plus, the mere *idea* of being in her presence makes me extremely nervous. So I

> Sometimes you meet your idols, and they don't live up to your expectations, but that moment was one of the best in my life.

chickened out. A few weeks later, I checked my mail and Barbra had sent me a copy of that night's program with a note on it that said: "Thank you for coming to my show, I wish you would have come backstage, I would have liked to have given you a hug." And then I really died.

A Few of My Favorite Things

Funny Girl: I love the story of a woman who struggles between love and her career. Plus, the music is just incredible.

Almost Famous: My parents grew up in a culture of concerts—they went to tons. And from that, my father has a deep classic rock obsession . . . Black Sabbath, Pink Floyd, the Who. This was the musical vocabulary of my childhood. *Almost Famous* really brings that era to life, and also just happens to have a great story and some incredible acting by Kate Hudson.

Jagged Little Pill: When I was first cast on Broadway, my mother took me to the Virgin Mega store to get me a gift for landing the role. I bought *Jagged Little Pill*, which changed my life: Alanis Morissette's voice felt and sounded like a different world—a world I had never heard before. It just resonated with my soul.

Spring Awakening: I know it's silly to say that a thing I happened to be involved with is one of my favorite things, but *Spring Awakening* was a huge part of my life from the ages of fourteen to twenty-two (more on this in the next chapter). I grew up with *Spring Awakening* and will always feel incredibly connected to the music. To this day, whenever I need some emotional therapy, I put on my headphones and listen to "And Then There Were None," "Blue Wind," and "Don't Do Sadness."

Les Misérables: Even if I hadn't been in *Les Mis,* I'd still think it's such an incredible musical.

The Light in the Piazza: I was desperate to be in this Broadway show, but I was deemed too ethnic to play the role of Clara. When I went to see it, I remember sitting in the audience and feeling like it was such an impressive example of why I do what I do.

Once: The music in *Once* is so incredible. When I was in Amsterdam in 2012, I walked around and listened to the soundtrack on repeat. The show (which was first a movie) is really the perfect package and is yet another example of the sort of piece that makes me proud to be an actor.

With Kate at the Glee season 4 premiere. Had the best time working with her on the show and feel so honored to now call this incredibly talented and strong woman a friend.

FAVORITE COMFORT FOOD

Italian Comfort Soup

This is a frill-free soup that's both healthy and comforting. It requires minimal work, too!

....

1. Cover the bottom of a pan with the olive oil and turn the heat to medium.

2. Add the carrots, celery, garlic, onion, and a pinch of salt and pepper and sauté until the vegetables are soft and tender, 5 to 8 minutes.

3. In a separate pot, bring the vegetable broth to a boil, then reduce the heat to low.

4. Add the sautéed vegetables to the broth and cook on low for 30 minutes.

5. Add a bit more salt and pepper, the red pepper flakes, and lemon juice to taste.

6. Add the potatoes and cook for 15 minutes.

7. Stir in the kale and lentils and cook for an additional 15 minutes.

8. Grate some Parmesan cheese (or vegan cheese) on top and serve!

3	tablespoons olive oil (enough to cover the bottom of the pot)
2 or 3	carrots, chopped
4	stalks celery, chopped
2 or 3	cloves garlic, minced
½	onion, chopped
4	cups organic vegetable broth
1 or 2	pinches of salt
1 or 2	pinches of pepper
4	cups organic vegetable broth
	Pinch of red pepper flakes (or to taste)
	Juice of 3 lemons
3 or 4	unpeeled russet potatoes, cubed
1	bunch kale, de-stemmed and chopped
2	15-ounce cans lentils
	Parmesan cheese, for serving

A WELL-ROUNDED LIFE

I spent a lot of time in the car when I was kid, ferrying between school and home, New Jersey and Broadway. It was exciting and wonderful but had its downsides, too, as I wasn't really able to forge deep relationships with friends. Everyone at school was nice and made room for me in their social groups when I was around, but after school, when it was prime socialization time, I was off to work. And in my community, Bar and Bat Mitzvahs were the end-all be-all—I made it to only a few of them. It was before those big nights that the girls got together and figured out what they were going to wear and how they were going to do their hair (which, funnily enough, usually involved flat-ironing all their gorgeous Jewish curls away), and it was at those parties that everyone let loose, that boys danced with girls, that memories were made. During the candle-lighting component of the event, the Bar Mitzvah boy, or Bat Mitzvah girl, would dedicate their candles to their closest friends. That could never be me: I wasn't on their sports teams, I wasn't hanging out at the mall with them after school, I wasn't cramming with them for math tests and English exams.

So my freshman year of high school, I decided to take a break from the stage and give myself a normal high school life. I just wanted to be on the volleyball team, and have a boyfriend, and hang out with my friends and family at night. I joined the debate team and became a

Sheila

MY IDEA OF A PERFECT SUNDAY

1. Make breakfast.
2. Go for a little hike in Runyon Canyon.
3. Go to the farmer's market.
4. Come home and watch the Food Network, specifically Diners, Drive-Ins and Dives and Chopped, with Sheila, the cat I found behind a dumpster on the Paramount lot.
5. Cook a nice dinner.
6. Watch a movie.

champion varsity debater, which still ranks as one of my most favorite things I've ever done. (In fact, it was so inspiring I seriously considered law school.) I tried debate for fun at first but teamed up with my friend Samantha, who was incredibly smart. Now, I was good at debate, but I wasn't very smart—and so my opponents would try to call me out by asking me to define words. Like *filibuster*. I was once asked to define *filibuster*. I had no clue what it meant, but I managed to debate my way out of it by accusing my opponent of using a spelling contest as a distraction from the fact that their case was false. I was the mouth on that team, while Samantha was the brains (she went on to be valedictorian). We won 90 percent of our debates, and not just because we dressed up to match and were cuter than our predominately male compatriots. We were just that good. I look back at my time on the debate team as one of my best memories of high school and the place where I picked up some skills that I still rely on today. I know that I can always argue myself out of sticky situations—and I'm never intimidated to go head-to-head with people, even if they're more educated than I am. It's been a great resource to have in my back pocket. When my agent called senior year to tell me that they were reprising *Fiddler on the Roof* and that while I wasn't fully Jewish, I was the most Jewish-looking girl in the business, I went back to Broadway. It broke my heart to abandon Samantha. I was devastated when Ben Shapiro replaced me as her partner. But ultimately, those three years of a normal high school life were all I needed to develop other interests.

I'm a huge fan of having a well-rounded life: During my formative years, it was important to me that I learn to excel at things outside of singing and acting. Not only did this give me a break from the business, but it reaffirmed that my heart belonged to the stage. And you should try other things without necessarily trying them out as your job; just because you love something doesn't mean it has to consume your days. It can just add richness and texture to your life. I spend most of my extracurricular time these days cooking, hiking, and catching up with my friends and family. Giving myself room to enjoy other things means that my passion for acting and singing never dulls.

In high school, when I looked back at my early days on Broadway, I discovered that the kids who were singularly focused on acting weren't in the business anymore. But the kids whose parents kept it light and fun and encouraged them to try other things are still working in theater today. No matter what those outside interests may be, they'll only enrich your life and make you better at your day job. For me, they make me a better actor, as they give me more to draw

GIVING MYSELF ROOM TO ENJOY OTHER THINGS MEANS THAT MY PASSION FOR ACTING AND SINGING NEVER DULLS.

upon and a wider frame of reference. Whether you want to get into show business or regular business, don't forget about the other things you enjoy doing, too. They won't take you away from your career—they'll just enrich your entire being. Nobody should be entirely defined by one thing.

HOW I STAY GROUNDED AND KEEP PERSPECTIVE

FAMILY

We all know that show business is very difficult, but based on what I've observed my friends go through, it seems that all business is pretty tough these days. There's always been pressure from traditional media to have a certain type of life and a certain amount of success, but with reality TV and social media joining the fray, there's just too much noise these days telling us what we should be doing and how we should be doing it. Or at least social media is telling us what everyone else is doing and how they're doing it. It can feel very overwhelming and confusing, particularly if your peers seem to be making bigger strides than you. It's very important to tune out the noise.

My mother and father were always the ones who reminded me that I should just be me. While other girls were partying it up and ending up facedown at the end of the night, I just wanted to get home. I refused to do what everyone else was doing just to be part of the crowd, particularly because when I was honest with myself, it didn't appeal to me at all. I thank my parents and extended family for giving me the strength to keep my head on straight and to stay focused on the things that are important to me. They've always been the support system that's allowed me to keep my eye on the prize. When my life starts to feel like it's spinning a bit out of control, or whenever I feel run-down, or exhausted, or like I can't possibly do it all, I always turn to them first. They always treat me like Lea Sarfati. In this business, it's very easy to forget who you are and where you come from, but they're a constant reminder that ultimately nothing has changed. Part of surviving Hollywood—and life, really—is to keep your world relatively intimate and packed with people who will always have your best interests in mind. My family is at the very center of the circle.

TAKING CARE OF MYSELF

My day job is physically and mentally pretty taxing: Besides the basics of being an actress (i.e., showing up on set with lines memorized), dancing and singing can really take their toll. I wouldn't be able to do any of it if I didn't put a premium on taking care of my body. If my schedule allows, a long hike or a yoga class reorients me—otherwise I'll always find five minutes to ride my bike around set, or five minutes just to sit and stretch. (I'll tell you more about this in chapter 5.) And ultimately, I love at-home centering, which is why you'll never find me letting off steam at bars or clubs, or shopping at the mall. The best remedy for a long day is always a thirty-minute bath.

When sensory overload strikes and I can't step away, I'll run through a quick meditation exercise. I close my eyes, tune out my surroundings, and just focus on taking deep breaths in through my nose and out through my mouth. Freaking out during a pop quiz or an overwhelming day at the office? I urge you to take a walk to the bathroom and try it.

And finally, I look for any opportunity to decompress. I grew up in a family where love is best expressed through food, so being in the kitchen is one of my favorite ways to unwind. My ultimate comfort food? Hearty soup or grilled cheese sandwiches—eaten while watching reality TV. Whether you find your calm through a delicious snack, a long run, or a phone call with a friend, don't let the stress of the outside world impose on your sense of perspective. Regardless of what it takes, make sure that you touch base, as often as possible, with all the things that make you you.

The Spotlight

1. Be you. It's so cheesy, but there's no one better at being you than you. Don't slough off the things that make you special just to fit a mold—your story is the most interesting thing you've got going for you, so use it!

2. Be proud of all the things that make you different, and flex those distinctions—where you come from and your family—as your biggest strengths.

3. Remember your role models and keep them in your mind as signposts for everything that's possible in life. Whether you're fifteen or fifty, it's always good to surround yourself with people you find inspiring and from whom you believe you can learn.

4. Keep the people who love you, like your family, close. They made you who you are, so don't neglect them on your road to achieving your goals. Assuming they're supportive, use them as a resource for strength and guidance. That's what they're there for!

5. Don't let stress derail you: Don't forget to check in with yourself every night.

↑ All smiles with my parents at the dinner table.

THE BIZ

"You have got to discover you, what you do, and trust it."
—BARBRA STREISAND

I've been collecting a paycheck since I was a little girl—doing jobs that seem too fun to be considered work. When I was eight, I landed on Broadway and started down the path to make my first childhood dream come true. No, I didn't want to be a princess, or a doctor, or even a member of the Mickey Mouse Club. I wanted to be a diva! It's funny that the word has negative connotations in Hollywood, because growing up, that was my dream! That's what every girl on Broadway strives to be. After all, didn't Beyoncé say that a diva is just a female version of a hustler? In New York, being a diva doesn't have negative connotations—it has great connotations. I wanted to live my life in stage makeup, in Times Square. I wanted to tackle all the famous Broadway roles, not only those played by its most famous leading ladies, either, but those played by the leading men, too. Because, quite frankly, why not? Any girl would want to play Maria from *West Side Story,* but what preteen fantasizes about playing Don Quixote in *Man of La Mancha?*

Once I found my place on Broadway, the passion and determination and motivation to make the stage my home forever took hold. I knew there was no other place for me to be, that I was lucky enough to find, at a very young age, exactly what I was good at and exactly what made me happy. And I intended to follow my heart and to keep performing—all with a smile on my face. Don't get me wrong: It wasn't always as easy as my first open audition when I was eight. After all, I wandered into that audition with no conception of how it would change my life—I only went because my best friend, Chloe, wanted to go, and somehow I ended up landing the role of Cosette on Broadway. I've definitely suffered my fair share of sucker-punch rejections and miscues: I've lost out on roles that I believed, at the time, were everything I needed to take the next step; I've lost count of the times that people who theoretically know all about these things told me I was making the wrong decisions (like the time that someone told me *Spring Awakening* would flop and I shouldn't do it, when it was actually one of the biggest catapults in my career—more on that later). But those bumps and burns only made me more thankful that I knew so deeply that I had found my true home, because I never for a second stopped pushing forward, thought about quitting, or ignored my own gut. I had the resolve to carry on, because nothing ever felt as right as performing, and I somehow knew that if I maintained my energy and enthusiasm and drive and sanity, and continued to work hard, I'd find my way through.

I've learned a lot of life skills on the stage along the way, which I will touch on in a few pages, but one of the most powerful lessons I learned is that you don't always get the jobs, and breaks, that you think you want and think you deserve. Just as you'll likely be passed over for a promotion at some point in your career, I've been passed over for a lot of roles. And while it always seemed like the end of the world, or at least the end of my career, in that moment, everything has always worked out for the best.

Case in point: I was devastated when I didn't land a part in the Broadway revival of *West Side Story,* as that's one of the shows I've always wanted to do, and I truly believed that would be my next big thing. It wasn't meant to be, and as tough as that was to fathom in the days after the rejection, a month later I got the part of Rachel Berry. As difficult as it can be to put your faith in the future, if you do your part by working hard and trying your best, I truly believe that good things will always come and the right path will make itself evident.

Whether you're considering a career on the stage or a career at a desk, I hope that it's a path you're so passionate about that you'll fight for every opportunity. I hope it sings to every fiber of your being and that you can't imagine doing anything else. Perhaps my job consumes a larger percentage of my life than that of the average person, but even forty hours a week is too many hours to spend doing something that makes you unhappy. And I would be a fool to suggest that happiness can be a constant state, particularly when it comes to work, but it should feel joyful at times, and fulfilling, and productive, and challenging as much as possible. You should feel like you're climbing a ladder that's worth climbing.

Here's a look at my career trajectory so far— and all the important lessons I've learned along the way. While these may seem to apply most directly to Broadway, I can't imagine that they wouldn't have prepped me for a normal day job, too.

LES MISÉRABLES (1995)

LESSONS LEARNED: BASIC PROFESSIONALISM AND OPTIMISM

BASIC PROFESSIONALISM

Les Misérables was the perfect introduction to what it means to have a job. I was one of three eight-year-old girls who played the parts of Young Cosette and Young Eponine: During the eight shows a week, we would rotate through those two roles and every third time become the understudy to the other two, in case someone got sick or otherwise couldn't perform.

Needless to say, I took to Broadway life like a fish to water, both the performing part and the job part. Sure, I had had a schedule before: a time to be at school, a time to go to bed. But I'd never been in a position where my actions affected other people directly. Quite simply, I had to behave. Because the show had been running on Broadway for a long time, they had a strong system in place for teaching us all the ropes of show business. I may have been precocious, but I really took that time to learn the seemingly simple rules of getting along in an adult world.

I immediately had to be professional, which on Broadway—and arguably beyond—means that I had to be on time; take care of myself and not get too tired or sick; and get along with, and work well with, others. It was very clear that we were each just one piece of a complex puzzle and that for the puzzle to come together correct-ly, we all had to do our part. I took all of this very seriously and absolutely loved being good at my job just as much as I loved playing with the other kids backstage. It was while doing *Les Misérables* that I learned that being the best at what you do and enjoying yourself while doing it are not mutually exclusive. That might seem like a silly lesson, but it's informed my entire career. Work can be fun!

And sure, we were eight years old; we definitely did our share of goofing around. Our story line took place at the beginning of the show, but we had to stick around for curtain call, so we took that time to literally play Broadway. While our peers might have been playing house, we were reen-acting *Miss Saigon* and *The Phantom of the Opera*. Clearly, we all loved the stage.

> IT WAS WHILE DOING *LES MISÉRABLES* THAT I LEARNED THAT BEING THE BEST AT WHAT YOU DO AND ENJOYING YOURSELF WHILE DOING IT ARE NOT MUTUALLY EXCLUSIVE. THAT MIGHT SEEM LIKE A SILLY LESSON, BUT IT'S INFORMED MY ENTIRE CAREER. WORK CAN BE FUN!

OPTIMISM

Like all the other kids in the cast, I wanted to be in *Les Misérables* forever. But all good things must end, and for kids on Broadway, things end

when you literally outgrow the part. We had to be measured every week: Some stage moms would teach their kids how to slouch, so they could stick around for a bit longer, but my parents always told me to stand up straight. They felt like I needed to learn that just because *Les Misérables* was amazing and fun didn't mean that there wouldn't be more amazing and fun things down the road. They always urged me to enjoy it while it lasted, with the understanding that there would be something great for me when it was over. It's hard to have that sort of faith when one show is all you've known and you've made great friends along the way, I would be lying if I didn't admit to crying my face off when I got the call that I had outgrown my role. But sure enough, two weeks later, I landed another part, where I learned some more important lessons.

→ Clockwise from top left: Little me—at around eight years old—doing a press appearance for Les Mis ✱ in my Young Éponine costume ✱ in character as Young Cosette ✱ singing at press events for Les Mis ✱ backstage in character as Young Cosette.

RAGTIME (1996–1999)

LESSONS LEARNED: THE CRAFT, TEAMWORK, AND PERSEVERANCE

THE CRAFT

While *Les Misérables* had already been running for almost ten years when I joined the cast in 1995, *Ragtime*, an early-twentieth-century period piece, was a newly developed show. As is the case with all new Broadway musicals, *Ragtime* required a yearlong trial run outside of New York City before making its Broadway debut. *Ragtime* would spend this year in Toronto. This was a very big deal for my family, as my mother had never left my father's side before, much less the country. But they thought it would be a great education for me, since I would get to work with four of Broadway's greats: Marin Mazzie, Brian Stokes Mitchell (who went on to play my father on *Glee*), Peter Friedman, and Audra McDonald.

My mother and I flew to Toronto and lived there for a year, and that is where I really learned about acting. I never had a singing or acting coach. I've taken a few classes from time to time, but for me, experience has always been the best way to learn. And in *Ragtime*, I was learning from the very best. Sure, I played my part, but what I really did was watch these four masters do their thing and absorb as much as possible. Every night, for example, I got to watch Audra McDonald sing her heart out: Every night, she would cry when she sang her song. Her ability to dig deep into her role, to tap into real emotions, to summon that character's backstory, was astounding. In one scene, Audra had an altercation with a police officer; backstage, before going on, she would ask that actor to berate her, so she could fully feel and express her character's pain and outrage. I watched her, and Brian, Marin, and Peter, practice their craft and soaked it all up like a sponge. Sometimes you just need to keep your mouth shut and learn.

Audra also taught me how to keep my mind centered on the job I needed to do onstage as Tateh's daughter, rather than the audience's reactions to my actions. One night near the beginning of the run, I was peeking out at the audience from behind the curtain. Audra tapped me on the shoulder and said, "If you can see them, they can see you—don't worry about the people out there, just focus on your role, focus on the show." And that's not all. Each evening before I would go onstage, Audra would put her hands around my waist and see how much I could expand my diaphragm. She taught me how to breathe; she

> ACCOUNTABILITY IS LITERALLY FRONT AND CENTER WHEN YOU'RE A STAGE ACTOR: THE AUDIENCE—WHO HAVE ALL PAID DEARLY FOR THEIR TICKETS—CAN TELL WHEN THE SHOW ISN'T WORKING. I NEEDED TO BE PREPARED EVERY DAY.

taught me the importance of saving my voice, of drinking tea and water, of refusing cigarettes. She always told me that my entire career would be contained between the bottom of my chin and the top of my diaphragm, that God had given me the gift of a voice, and it was my responsibility to take care of it.

TEAMWORK

In *Ragtime*, I played Peter Friedman's daughter, and so we were pretty much inseparable throughout the show. This was new for me, since I'd never worked so intensely with another actor. I couldn't be off at any time during that show without directly affecting him. Accountability is literally front and center when you're a stage actor: The audience—who have all paid dearly for their tickets—can tell when the show isn't working. I needed to be prepared every day. I owed it to Peter and to all the people who came to see us perform. I took a night off once and my understudy went on in my stead. After, Peter asked me not to take any more breaks. Sure, that sounds extreme, but it underlines how dependent our performances were on each other. And quite frankly, I was relieved and thankful that I was missed; I was young and territorial about my roles. In fact, when I got *Ragtime*, they pulled my mother aside and asked her about the possibility of rotating the role between me and another girl, and even though I was only ten, and arguably too young to be negotiating my own contract,

I jumped right in and told them that I was ready to perform every night—and that if they wanted me, I was doing it by myself. So when Peter told me that he didn't want me to miss any more performances, it was really another way of saying, "Job well done."

PERSEVERANCE

After our year in Canada was up, we brought the show to Broadway, which felt like an entirely different place than when I had been on Broadway in *Les Misérables*. Since it was a brand-new show, we were reviewed by the critics, we performed on talk shows, and we eventually performed at the Tony Awards, which are the be-all and end all of Broadway life.

During *Ragtime*, I learned another very important life lesson, which is that passion can, and should, trump what people say. At the time I wasn't aware of Ben Brantley (the chief theater critic for the *New York Times*), I just knew that I loved and believed in the show, and no review—good or bad—was going to change my opinion of my job. (The reviews of *Ragtime* were mixed.) My dedication and devotion to *Ragtime* far exceeded anything that anyone could ever say about it. Sure, I was blissfully young at the time, and much of what was happening was over my head (there were lots of politics involving the investors in the show that I was not tuned in to), but learning to let criticism and outside opinions—both good and bad—glance off me is

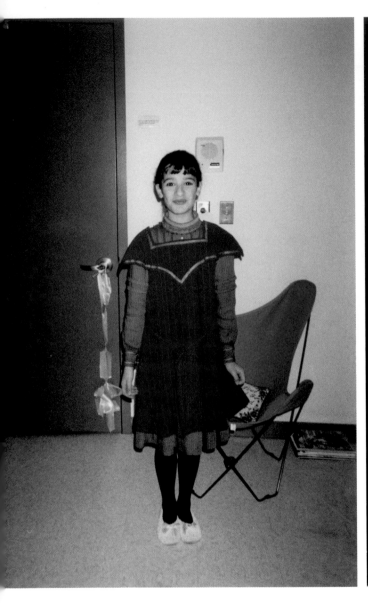

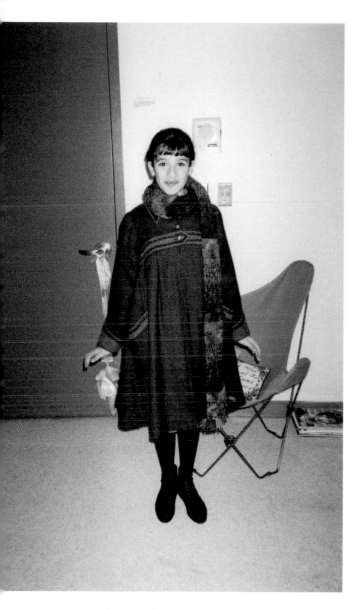

a lesson I still lean on today. Of course feedback is important and should always be considered, but constructive criticism is very different from straight-up opinion. I listened to the director, I listened to my castmates, and most important, I listened to my heart—and then I kept on trying my best.

I went to the Tony Awards with Peter Friedman that year as his guest; he was nominated for best actor in a musical. I wanted him to win so badly—more than anything in the world—but he lost. I was much more upset than he was when his name wasn't called, and he turned to me and said, "Lea, it's okay." It wasn't the end of the world for him, and it didn't change the fact that he was proud of his work. Audra won a Tony that year, but everyone else—Brian, Peter, Marin—lost. Even though they lost, they still went on every night and did an amazing show; even when there was no prize left, they still acted their hearts out.

I was in *Ragtime* for two years. The original cast left the show in one night, a passing of the torch, which is standard practice on Broadway. Working with those actors was an incredible experience; watching them every night was my master class, my Juilliard.

↑ Left to right: Backstage at <u>Ragtime</u>, dressed up as the little girl ✱ with the incredible Marin Mazzie and my other young costar in <u>Ragtime</u> ✱ backstage at <u>Ragtime</u>.

FIDDLER ON THE ROOF (2004)

LESSONS LEARNED: FOCUS AND PATIENCE

FOCUS

When I left *Ragtime*, I was just finishing the eighth grade. Perfect timing, because I couldn't have been more excited to start high school. I spent the first three years focused on having a relatively normal schedule and life. As we've discussed, I needed a chance to take my own pulse and develop interests outside of acting—if only to reaffirm that it was what I really wanted to do. Senior year, life on the stage called again, and I went back to Broadway. I took a part in *Fiddler on the Roof* in 2004 and balanced that final year between school and work.

Fiddler was a totally different experience for me for many reasons: For one, it was a smaller part, and for another, I was no longer a child. My mom didn't take me to work anymore. In fact, I got my own apartment in the city and started to feel that my life was really up to me—that I had to do it on my own. While I had a principal role in *Fiddler* as Daughter #4, it wasn't a huge part, and I had to share a dressing room with about twelve other women, who ranged in age from nineteen to sixty. Most people start out in an ensemble or chorus, but I had been lucky enough to only land featured roles up to that point, where I had my own private space to get ready and focus my mind. This wasn't to be on *Fiddler*, and I had to quickly adjust to less-than-ideal circumstances. Sharing a room was an education in every sense of the word, and while I can't say it was fun or that I enjoyed it, I'm glad I experienced it. Whether you're in an office or backstage, it's important to be able to quiet your mind even in the midst of tumult. All of the women had their own process, their own drama, their own pre-show rituals, and I had to adjust without letting the extra noise derail me from my performance. It took a lot of concentration every day to ignore everything that was happening around me, since it's imperative that I engage 100 percent with my job so that I can do my very best.

PATIENCE

In *Fiddler*, besides playing the part of Daughter #4, I was the understudy to the much larger role of Daughter #3 (the first three daughters had the lion's share of lines, while Daughter #4 and Daughter #5 said very little). As an under-

> AS AN UNDERSTUDY, YOU HAVE TO BE PREPARED TO GO ON EVERY NIGHT, THOUGH GOING ON RARELY COMES TO PASS. AND THAT'S HARD, BECAUSE YOU WANT TO PLAY THAT ROLE ALL THE TIME BUT HAVE TO HANG OUT IN THE WINGS AND WATCH SOMEONE ELSE DO IT INSTEAD.

study, you have to be prepared to go on every night, though going on rarely comes to pass. And that's hard, because you want to play that role all the time but have to hang out in the wings and watch someone else do it instead. I really loved and respected Tricia Paoluccio, the girl for whom I understudied, but that doesn't mean it wasn't challenging to not be in the spotlight—opposite Alfred Molina, no less—every night. As was my luck, Tricia *never* called in sick. The one time I got to go on was when she was on vacation. I was so incredibly nervous that I doused myself in lavender oil to calm my nerves; while I was sitting on the side of the stage prepping myself to go on, I heard someone exclaim, "What the hell is that smell?" I turned to them and apologized, and they said, "You smell like a tea bag!"

Ultimately, I left *Fiddler* because as nice as it was to collect a paycheck, I wasn't getting enough out of the experience creatively—I needed to grow and stretch my muscles a bit more. The character of Daughter #4 didn't have much of an arc, and as an actor, it started to feel a little dull—I was anxious to take on more.

↑ Left to right: The Broadway revival cast of *Fiddler on the Roof* ✱ me in my Shprintze, aka Daughter #4, costume.

SPRING AWAKENING (2000-2008)

LESSONS LEARNED: CONVICTION
AND EMOTIONAL HARDINESS

CONVICTION

Immediately after *Ragtime*, I auditioned for a role in a workshop for a new play called *Spring Awakening*. A workshop is pretty much exactly that: Before a play can get the investors it needs to make it to Broadway, the creators put up a production to massage out all the play's kinks. The script morphs, the actors come and go, and the play ultimately (and hopefully) finds its footing. We did four workshops for *Spring Awakening* over the span of five years (from age fourteen to nineteen for me), until it finally landed an off-Broadway run in New York City in 2005.

That was a big moment, since we'd all invested a huge amount of time and energy into seeing the show get off the ground. At that point, it was *already* a profound part of my life. When I got the call that we had made it to off Broadway I was in the hospital with my mother, who was recovering from surgery for uterine cancer. Needless to say, it was a very emotional day.

And it was emotional, too, because I believed wholeheartedly in the show. I always had a feeling about *Spring Awakening*. It was such a unique and powerful piece, and the character I got to play was so strong and unusual. *Spring Awakening* is about children exploring their sexuality in Germany in the late nineteenth century. My role

changed considerably from when I did the workshops at age fourteen (kissing and innuendo) to when I was nineteen (full-on simulated sex), to the point that I eventually got a Post-it in my dressing room that simply stated, "We should see your breasts," from the director, Michael Mayer. I was excited to do this, quite honestly, because I loved challenging the people in the audience who found it uncomfortable. I did have a clause in my contract, though, that I never had to do it when my dad was in the audience.

Besides the subject matter, the music was *incredible*. Duncan Sheik wrote it (I still have the CD of him singing all the songs, which was delivered along with the original script), and it sounded like a cross between Radiohead and the Beatles. While *Rent* had broken some ground, this really was a completely new sound for Broadway. Funnily, at my audition, they asked me to sing a pop song, but I was a musical-theater kid—the only song I knew was Jessica Simpson's "I Think I'm in Love with You," which I had heard on the radio. Thanks to my years on *Glee,* I know a lot more pop songs now!

We opened in 2005 to great reviews, which wasn't surprising since we had a cast of really talented kids: Jonathan Groff, Jon Gallagher, Lauren Pritchard . . . the list goes on and on. And like with *Glee,* which we'll talk about in a later chapter, the show rode entirely on the backs of those kids. One day, when we were in tech rehearsal, which is when you run through the play again and again and again to set the lighting, I was sitting up in the balcony of the Eugene O'Neill Theatre with Lauren Pritchard watching the goings on. She turned to me and said, "Lea, what are we going to do if this show doesn't make it?" and then was promptly called to the stage to do one of her songs, which was a really beautiful number called "Blue Wind." I sat up there and I watched her, and I got chills. When she came back up to the balcony after, I looked at her and I said, "Lauren, if you do that every night, we're going to be just fine."

And we were more than fine. While we opened the show in a tiny church in Chelsea, we were soon on Broadway and eventually found ourselves the stars of one of the season's biggest success stories. In many ways, it was the perfect training ground for *Glee,* though on a much smaller scale, and like with *Glee,* those kids in the cast became my best friends and, essentially, my family. It wasn't just a showmance—our bonds were very real.

EMOTIONAL HARDINESS

If you haven't seen it, *Spring Awakening* is a very intense play to both watch and perform. What we went through on that stage was very, very hard and emotional, and it called on all of us to dig deep eight shows a week. Spoiler alert, but the character I played, Wendla, is young, precocious, and strong, and over the course of the show she goes through a lot. There's a very intense beating scene, there's a very intense sex scene, and ultimately Wendla dies from a botched abortion at the end of the play. It wasn't easy stuff. There were days when I really didn't want to go there emotionally; drawing upon those feelings every night so I could make Wendla come alive was truly exhausting. But doing that show again and again gave me stamina, and it taught me how to really access my emotions. I was going through a lot of personal stuff at the time—I was in a relationship that had its ups and downs—and so to do the show, I had to put that aside. That was an important lesson: No matter what, the show must go on. There are 1,100 people who have paid to see you perform, and you have to do your best. If the turmoil in my daily life wasn't something that I could harness and use on the stage, then I left everything that was going on in the dressing room. I could never afford to let it affect the show in a negative way.

IF YOU HAVEN'T SEEN IT, *SPRING AWAKENING* IS A VERY INTENSE PLAY TO BOTH WATCH AND PERFORM. WHAT WE WENT THROUGH ON THAT STAGE WAS VERY, VERY HARD AND EMOTIONAL, AND IT CALLED ON ALL OF US TO DIG DEEP EIGHT SHOWS A WEEK.

IN SHORT . . .

Spring Awakening won eight Tony Awards and a Grammy, which was pretty amazing validation for the work we were doing. And it was perfect prep for what came next. We'll talk more about *Glee*, but it's safe to say that I never would have landed that role without all the work of the years before—both onstage and off—which really taught me the skills I needed to succeed in the business. And quite frankly, probably in any business. In *Les Misérables*, I learned the basics of having and holding a job; in *Ragtime*, I learned a ton about acting, as well as teamwork and being accountable for doing my part well; in *Fiddler*, I learned that you don't always get what you want and sometimes must be patient; and in *Spring Awakening*, I learned how to balance my personal and professional lives and really dig deep to access my emotions. I know that I don't have the typical day job, but I hope—and think—that these are skills that are pretty easy to apply to *any* type of career. Ultimately, it's about being part of a team, learning on the job, and always trying to do your best.

OWNING YOUR ACCOMPLISHMENTS

We live in a world of self-deprecation, and while it's healthy to make fun of ourselves from time to time, it bothers me when I see women of all ages belittling their accomplishments because they don't want to appear boastful or overconfident. You don't see a lot of guys out there underplaying their strengths or making light of what they're good at, so why should women? While I get that there's a fine line between owning your accomplishments and reciting every line of your résumé, there is absolutely no shame in being proud of what you've managed to achieve! Own it!

The Other Things I've Learned Along the Way . . .

FAKE IT 'TIL YOU MAKE IT

When my dad is asked if he can do something, his standard response is, "Sure I can do it—of course I can do it!" regardless of what the "it" might be. As I mentioned, my dad *hustles*. Like father, like daughter, because I've done the same thing my entire life—sometimes to my detriment. I auditioned for the musical *Brigadoon* and after I sang for Rob Ashford, the director, he stopped me as I was leaving the room and asked, "Lea, how's your extension?" I had no clue what he meant, so just responded, "It's great!" He then asked me if I could do the splits, to which I replied, "Of course!" I couldn't do the splits, but I wasn't going to shoot myself in the foot unnecessarily. I figured I'd just muddle my way through. A few weeks later, I had a dance callback for the show, and I couldn't do any of it: I thoroughly embarrassed myself in this room full of ballerinas who *did* have incredible extension. They were leaping across the room in perfect arcs, while I looked like a skit straight out of *Saturday Night Live*. It was hilarious but still worthwhile: I just don't believe in admitting preemptive defeat, particularly if there's any chance to learn on the job. Inevitably, I wasn't cast in the show, but at least I didn't limit myself. I always think it's better to scramble to learn a new skill than to sell yourself short.

FREQUENTLY ASKED FAN QUESTIONS

Your burning questions about the business answered!

Q HOW DO YOU DEAL WITH AUDITION NERVES?

A I prepare for auditions probably as much as everyone else prepares for a job interview. Ultimately, so long as I do my best in the room, the decision about whether I get the job or not really isn't up to me, so to ease my nerves (I still get very, very nervous prior to auditions), I try to control as much about the experience as possible. By that I mean that I've researched the role, read the script, gone to see the show (if the show already exists), picked my music, practiced my music, practiced my lines, printed my music out, and figured out where the audition is and exactly how long it's going to take me to get there. I leave nothing to chance. Ultimately, the more I know what I'm going to do when I get into that room, the less nervous I tend to be. That way, when audition day rolls around, I can stay calm and focused, knowing in the back of my mind that I've done everything humanly possible to prepare.

Because I've crossed all my *T*s and dotted all my *I*s, on the day of the actual audition I keep things calm and light. I get up, get ready, and go. And I try to keep things calm and light in the room, too, so that if something does go wrong, it's easier to laugh it off and move forward. I've had auditions where I've completely forgotten my lines—it happens to everyone. The best thing to do is to make something out of it and make them laugh: They'll certainly remember you! And if you don't get the role, don't despair. There will *always* be opportunities, and there will always be more auditions.

Q HOW DO YOU HANDLE DIFFICULT COWORKERS?

A We've all been there, where we've had to work with someone who might not be the easiest to deal with on a day-to-day basis. My trigger is feeling like I'm prepared and others aren't—that's very, very frustrating, particularly because it affects not only the cast but the entire crew, too, who are there to do their jobs well and go home. It's also frustrating when people are unprofessional or bring their personal life, or drama, to set. Over the years, I've learned that the best thing to do is to literally block it from my mind and to resist the urge to obsess over the injustice of it all or fixate on their missteps. Ultimately, you can't control other people.

At times, I've felt that situations have become unworkable, and since I tend to be honest and direct, I've found that addressing the problem with my coworker face-to-face works best. If there's a situation that's causing tension, I'm known for giving a big hug to break the ice—usually, by offering that it's been a long week and that maybe we can start fresh, it's possible to clear the air. When you're onstage, or filming, with someone, it's very personal, and it goes much better when you have a good relationship. When a good relationship just isn't possible, I do my best to be civil so that I can move forward without friction or distraction.

Q HOW DO YOU KEEP A WORK/LIFE BALANCE?

A I learned at a young age that when my personal life is good, then my work is at its best. So even though I theoretically work all the time, and that work would seem to be my priority, the opposite is actually true. I prize my alone time and cherish my family and friends. Without a full and good personal life, I'd be terrible at my job: It all makes me a bigger and better actor. I keep potential chaos in check by being pretty old-school: I keep a physical calendar. I write everything down in my day planner so that I can be sure that my days are balanced, that I'm doing things that genuinely make me happy, and that I'm not just socializing to keep myself busy. I also try to make sure that I put my phone down when I'm with the people I love, in order to be fully present and focused on the time that I have with them.

Q WHAT WOULD YOU DO IF YOU COULDN'T ACT?

A For a while, I really wanted to practice law; I was on the debate team and it was such a fun experience, so I figured making my case in front of a jury would be just as fun. But the reality is that I was born a singer, and singing is what I do best.

Q WHAT WOULD YOU DO IF YOUR FAMILY DIDN'T SUPPORT YOU, BUT YOU KNEW ACTING WAS WHAT YOU WANTED YOU TO DO?

A It's hard for me to conceive of what it would be like if my family didn't support my choice to be in show business, but I do know a lot of people whose families really want them to pick careers with more stability. Working as an actor can be very unpredictable, and I think it's understandable that a lot of parents just want their kids to be able to pay their rent every month. What makes it even more confusing is that a lack of a steady income says nothing about someone's talent: I know some of the most talented people in the world who have trouble getting acting jobs. It can be very hard to reconcile those two facts, since I think we'd all like to believe that if you've got the talent, you'll get paid to do it. Unfortunately, it's not always that simple. I totally get why a parent would want their child to land a weekly paycheck, but if acting is going to make you happier than a reliable income, acting is what you must do!

A BEST: Work hard at what you love, and love what you do. If it makes you happy, go for it 100 percent. And, as Audra told me, if you've been given a gift, it's your responsibility to honor it and use it well.

WORST: To change my appearance. That might have ended my career since not looking like the other girls is what sets me apart!

THE SPOTLIGHT

These are the tools that have been most helpful in my career. Though I've never had a more traditional day job, my friends who aren't in show business think they apply in the real world, too.

1. PROFESSIONALISM: While getting a great role is a dream come true, at the end of the day, it's a job, and it requires hard work. I take professionalism very seriously: I'm always on time, I try my best while I'm there, and I stay until we're done without complaining.

2. FOCUS, DETERMINATION, AND DRIVE: Like with any career path where big opportunities and promotions are at stake, there are a lot of ups and downs in show business: You have to be able to take your lumps and still keep your eye on the prize. Whether you get an amazing part or fail to get a callback, whether you get nominated for an award or passed over, you have to stay focused.

3. AMIABILITY: Just like anyone on an interdependent team at the office, when you're an actor, you work *very* closely with other people; it's crucial that you find ways to relate to them. Long days are much more fun when the atmosphere is friendly. In short, it's basic office politics: Be genuinely kind to everyone, and they'll look out for you. Plus, you never know where people are going to end up: The young assistant will very likely be a powerful producer someday; the intern might eventually become your agent; that receptionist might be interviewing you someday. I always treat everyone with respect, in the same way that I would want to be treated.

4. DEDICATION TO THE CRAFT: I don't know any great actor who ever feels like they're as good as they could be. A willingness and interest to learn and grow is crucial: After all, every new role requires you to harness something different. Likewise, my friends who work in the real world are constantly looking to develop their skills. Besides doing the job they currently have, they always grab the initiative to take on any additional work that might teach them something new.

5. CULTIVATE STRONG CONNECTIONS:
This is important both on and off the screen and stage. Just as you need to be able to convey story and emotion to the audience, you need to be able to connect with casting directors and producers backstage. Ultimately, it's all about being memorable: While the job you're interviewing for or the role you're trying to land might not be right, there's always the chance that the casting director or recruiter will recommend you for something else.

6. TOUGHNESS. The more people pay attention to you, the more they'll have to say—and some of the things they'll say won't be nice. You have to learn how to focus on what's important and quiet the doubt inside.

7. ENERGY: When you're acting, you're essentially "on" all the time. This requires a huge amount of energy. Taking proper care of yourself definitely helps in this regard!

8. OPEN-MINDEDNESS AND FLEXIBILITY:
Unless you're an acting/directing/producing single-man show, you need to be able to take direction and orders from others. Sometimes they know best (see number 4).

9. SUPPORT: This is a tough but wonderful business that would likely feel completely overwhelming without the support of family and

When you're acting, you're essentially "on" all the time. This requires a huge amount of energy. Taking proper care of yourself definitely helps in this regard!

friends. Don't forget about them while you're pursuing your dreams!

10. PASSION: Hopefully, your career will be your career for a long time. If you don't love it, it's probably not worth pursuing, and it probably won't be sustainable.

SELF-
CARE 101

"You think beautiful girls are going to stay in style forever? I should say not! Any minute now they're going to be out! Finished! Then it'll be my turn!"
—FANNY BRICE, *FUNNY GIRL*

My job requires a huge amount of energy—much like any career that involves being "on." As you can imagine, playing a character like Rachel Berry is no joke. In order to show up to work refreshed and rested so that I can act my heart out, it's imperative that I capitalize on my downtime and do things for myself that feel energizing and indulgent. Like most actresses, I spend a lot of time in the hair and makeup chair getting prepped for on-camera work, but while getting primped by the pros seems like a wonderful luxury, it's not the same as a great at-home spa session. Maybe it's *because* I spend so much time at the hands of others, but I'll take self-pampering over a trip to a fancy spa any day.

I think this is in part because when I whip up a face masque in the kitchen or put something restorative on my hair before I sit down to watch TV, I'm literally taking care of myself—and psychically, that's how I prepare myself to tackle long days on set and in the studio. Sure, I'm not as qualified as a professional aesthetician, but I would still argue that we can take better care of ourselves than anyone else. Plus, it's a lot less expensive than booking a massage at a spa. I really prize this time both for my sanity and also for my health.

Beyond this ritual's therapeutic effects, I just cannot neglect my skin. I've been on Accutane twice. In fact, you know those kids who become nearly suicidal about their acne? I've walked that fine line. It was impossible at times to look beyond my pimple-ridden skin or to imagine a time when I wouldn't have to spackle my face just to leave my bedroom. Hilariously, I thought I had picked up a great concealing trick from *Sex and the City,* when Carrie uses a black eyeliner to turn a zit into a beauty mark. Brilliant, except my skin was so bad I needed about sixteen beauty marks. I went out with my girlfriends with black dots all over my face thinking I had the world fooled. They took one look at me and asked, "What . . . did you do to your face?"

It took years—and a truly excellent dermatologist—to get my skin to a point where it has calmed down. Knowing how it's capable of behaving, and having gone through what I've gone through, I now give my skin the best care possible. I use good products, I keep regular appointments with my dermatologist, and since I spend a majority of my days in heavy stage makeup (and a seemingly equal number of nights on the road), whenever I can, I give my skin a vacation. Plus, it's nice to remember what I actually look like, which can be difficult when I spend so much of each day looking at myself through an inch of foundation.

Back when I didn't have any money, buying products to test-drive at home was really hard on my wallet—these days, I can thankfully afford the skin care I really need, but I still like to add some home-brewed, all-natural concoctions to the mix. Whenever I opt to stay in, I catch up with my mom or my friends on the phone while lathering on pimple cream and applying all sorts of restorative gunk to my hair. That's what alone time is for!

And I don't need an entire evening alone to pamper myself, either—I have all sorts of bedtime rituals that really help me sleep better. At times, we have seventeen-hour days on the set of *Glee,* and when I finally get home, I only want to crash (sleep is the ultimate luxury, after all), but if I take the extra thirty seconds to put a hair masque on before I go to bed or rub some eucalyptus oil on my scalp, when I wake up to go to work a few short hours later, I feel refreshed. The more I'm being hammered on the work front, the more essential it is to show myself some love. It really is about the little things: A quick face or hair masque or exfoliation before I hit the sheets helps me reset—and quickly erases, or even just wraps up, a hard day. I urge you— whether you're still in school cramming for finals or spending your days in an office—to find every opportunity to pamper yourself (there's nothing to stop you from putting on a masque while you finish your work, or take care of chores around the house, or, you know, catch up on a few episodes of *Scandal*). It doesn't cost a lot of money to truly indulge and create a luxurious experience in your own home.

DRINK MORE WATER!

I know you've heard this a
hundred times (water and
sunscreen always top lists of
beauty must-dos), but I still
insist on claiming this as one
of the most important weapons
in my beauty tool kit. Being a
singer, it's essential that I
guzzle water, but the other
benefit is that it's so good for
my skin, too. Between juice,
soda, coffee . . . it's so easy
to forget to actually drink
old-fashioned water, and whenever I feel especially tired or
have a headache, I realize that
it's because I've been drinking
everything *but* water for the
past twenty-four hours. When
I'm on set at *Glee*, I'll bring
four huge bottles, and I vow
that I won't leave set that night
until I've finished all of them.
I guzzle water down the same
way a frat boy might funnel
a six-pack of beer. To make it
more interesting, I add fresh
mint leaves, cucumbers, lemon,
or fresh fruit like strawberries
or raspberries.

epsom salt

essential oils

baking soda

mustard bath

potpourri

BATH AND SHOWER ESSENTIALS

Taking the time to take a bath is one of my biggest indulgences—but they really do make me feel and look so much better. I like to concoct different combinations of oils and salts based on what I need, whether it's to soften my skin, relax after a stressful day, or ease aching muscles. When I don't have time for a full-on bath, I'll use essential oils in the shower just to make it a little special. These ingredients are the basis for my bath-time ritual. I soak for at least fifteen minutes. I like to download meditation tracks from iTunes and listen to them while I'm in the tub; they enhance the whole experience and make it even more relaxing.

RELAXATION AND ACHING MUSCLES: One heaping cup of Epsom salt + a few drops of lavender oil (to your liking)

SKIN SOFTENING: One scoop of mustard bath (Try Dr. Singha's Natural Therapeutics Mustard Bath. It's a mixture of ground mustard seeds and herbs.) + a few drops of tea tree oil (it's also really good for your scalp if you want to massage a few drops in)

STRAIGHT-UP DETOX AND PH BALANCE: Half a 1-pound box of baking soda (I've built up to an entire box, but use a smaller amount to start!)

MY BIG-TIME NO-NOS

These are the things I will never—under any circumstances—do. Some of these are basic common sense, while others have been drilled into me by the pros I work with routinely.

1. SLEEP WITH MY MAKEUP ON OR SKIP WASHING MY FACE BEFORE BED. As tired as I sometimes am at the end of the day, I never, ever skip this step. When you leave your makeup on, you're essentially tucking it into your pores and inviting a pimple over for a slumber party.

2. USE DIRTY BRUSHES OR OLD MAKEUP. I toss my makeup every three months and wash my brushes even more frequently. I use a spray intended specifically for washing them, but you can also clean brushes with a very gentle shampoo (just make sure to rinse them well). In order to waste as little as possible, I keep my makeup bag nice and streamlined.

3. USE OTHER PEOPLE'S PRODUCTS. Even if you're convinced your friends don't have any communicable diseases, we all have our own unique set of germs, which aren't great to share (particularly if you have acne-prone skin like me).

4. SHORT MYSELF ON SLEEP. I really need eight hours.

5. FLY WITH MAKEUP ON. If I'm having a bad skin day or know that I'll be encountering the paparazzi at the airport, I'll put on makeup and then remove it all as soon as I board the plane. I always carry wipes with me. I use this time in the sky to pamper my skin and really let it breathe (see opposite for my crazy rituals).

6. NOT DRINK ENOUGH WATER (ESPECIALLY WHEN FLYING). As mentioned, I make a conscientious effort to get as much down my throat as possible throughout the day.

7. SLEEP ON DIRTY PILLOWCASES. I change my sheets every week. During the summer, I'll swap them out even more frequently.

8. PUT MAKEUP ON AFTER FACIALS. I book a facial when I can tell my skin really needs to be cleaned out—and during that process, they open up all of your pores. It's really important to let your skin breathe and heal for as long as possible.

9. TOUCH MY FACE WITH DIRTY HANDS! In fact, I try not to touch my face at all—and I definitely never pick at it!

10. SKIP SUNSCREEN. My friend Jonathan Groff never really thought to protect his skin from the sun—after all, he's not an avid tanner and didn't think he was at risk. But crazily enough, he went to the doctor and was diagnosed with skin cancer. What's scarier is that his doctor told him that if it had gone unchecked, he could have been dead within a few months. The cancer was removed and he's okay now, but he made me promise to have my moles checked. Even though I'm naturally dark and not inclined to burn, thanks to Jonathan I always, always wear sunscreen: I slather SPF 50 on my face and SPF 20 on my body, and go in for mole checks religiously. Even if you don't live in sunny L.A., protect your skin from the sun!

TRAVELING TIPS

I always keep a travel kit prepped and packed. That way, if I know I'm not going to be sleeping in my own bed that night, I have everything I need on hand. As mentioned, I never, ever use other people's products or products supplied by hotels—it doesn't matter if they're the nicest products around. Coming from a place of having bad skin, I know that I must stick with what works best and avoid stressing my skin out by changing my routine. Some people are blessed to be able to use anything they want—or to skip washing their face entirely—but I am just not that lucky! If I have sample sizes of all my go-tos with me wherever I go, then I never have to stress out about something possibly making me break out. Whole Foods has a great aisle of organic, travel-size beauty products; Kiehl's is a great resource, too. These are the products that are always with me—with the exception, perhaps, of your razor and hair bands, keeping consistent to your brand of choice is really important:

1. FACE WASH
2. MOISTURIZER
3. PIMPLE CREAM
4. A RAZOR
5. HAIR BANDS
6. SHAMPOO
7. CONDITIONER

MAKING THE MOST OF IN-FLIGHT TIME

I love traveling with my makeup artist, Melanie Inglessis, because we've developed all sorts of rituals and routines to pass the time—and do great things for our skin in the process. After we've settled in and the plane has taken off, we clean our faces with rosewater-soaked pads and apply a heavy moisturizer to help counteract how dehydrating in-flight air can be on the skin. We also slather on yummy lip balm.

Melanie always packs full-face and collagen eye masques, which she applies to both of us when we're ready to fall asleep. Everyone looks at us like we're crazy, but it's 100 percent worth it. What's better than landing with gorgeous and refreshed skin?

Once we wake up, we remove the masques, wipe off the extra with cotton pads, and use an astringent toner to close our pores.

Next, we apply a light moisturizer and a little bit of eye cream (tap it on with your ring finger in a circular motion around the socket of the eye). Then we finish our faces with a tinted moisturizer to create a healthy and even glow, a bit of concealer for blemishes, and some powder in the T-zone area, and we're ready to deplane! Melanie doesn't wear much makeup, but sometimes I apply a bright red lip, which is my go-to look when the rest of my face is bare.

FULL SPA DAY RITUAL (IN MY OWN BATHROOM)

When I have the luxury of time and an unscheduled morning or afternoon, I'll pull out all the stops and focus my energy on pampering rituals. Not only is it a quick ticket to centering and reconnecting with myself, but it absolutely makes my hair and skin—not to mention soul!—look and feel better.

FIRST, I draw a restorative bath, usually one that eases muscle aches, particularly if I've had a very strenuous week on set or workout.

SECOND, I apply a restorative hair masque. Because my hair is being curled and blown out con-

stantly, my ends tend to get dry, so my hair guru, Mark Townsend, taught me this recipe—you can get the ingredients at a health food shop or grocery store like Whole Foods. When I'm really lucky, he whips it up for me and hands me a jar to stash in my shower. The heat from the water liquefies the coconut, which is key—but because the ingredients separate, you'll want to give it a vigorous shake before you apply. For his clients who have fine hair, Mark instructs them to dilute the mixture with water and store it in the shower in a spray bottle so they can mist it on very lightly. Again, you have to shake it vigorously to remix the ingredients before spritzing it on your ends—and then just leave it for a few minutes before washing it out so it doesn't weigh hair down. He likes me to leave this in my hair for an hour every week (I wrap it up in a shower cap).

Mark's Hair Masque

1 cup coconut oil (an excellent moisturizer composed of tiny molecules—molecules so tiny, in fact, that they can penetrate the shaft of the hair)

1 tablespoon almond oil (essential fatty acids)

1 tablespoon jojoba oil (moisturizer)

1 teaspoon vitamin E oil (lubricant)

1 teaspoon carrot oil (only use a drop or two if you're blond, since it can stain hair)

carrot oil

almond oil

coconut oil

vitamin e oil

jojoba oil

THIRD, I drain the tub and stay seated while I exfoliate my entire body with a scrub. **For an intense, hard scrub,** I'll take a bowl and mix two scoops of Epsom salt with five tablespoons of olive oil until it's the right consistency (make sure the olive oil is thoroughly mixed). **For a medium-intense scrub,** I'll take a bowl and mix two scoops of brown sugar with about two table-spoons of either honey or agave (agave is not as thick). Again, you want to make sure that the honey or agave is blended with the brown sug-ar, though it should still feel coarse. **For a light scrub,** I'll mix two scoops of coconut oil (micro-wave it if it's too difficult to stir) with twice as much sugar and a bit of fresh lime or lemon peel. Alternately, there are loads of great premade or-ganic scrubs at Whole Foods.

FOURTH, after my skin is nice and soft, I rinse off in the shower and wash my hair.

FIFTH, I apply Dr. Hauschka's Rose Body Oil everywhere except for my face. It's luxurious but doesn't cost a fortune (you can get it online) and moisturizes my skin better than anything else.

SIXTH, I apply a face masque. A frozen cucum-ber version is my absolute go-to since it calms my skin down considerably—it's really great for all skin types. I leave this on until it starts to melt and then rinse with cool water. (Keep in mind that it can get messy!)

Cucumber Face Masque

Take two chopped cucumbers and a hand-ful of ice and blend until it's the consistency of a thick puree (it's kind of like a slushy). I add a few drops of peppermint oil and then apply it quickly before it melts. When I have time, I ring the edge of my face with strips of cotton to prevent it from getting every-where; when I'm in a rush, I'll just apply it to the eye area. It's *freezing* but feels amazing.

SEVENTH, I do a quick at-home mani/pedi. Depending on how much time has passed since I got out of the tub, I soak my feet in hot water with a little eucalyptus or peppermint oil and then soften my soles up with a buffer. I then apply a coat of nail strengthener and some thick lotion.

My Relaxation Must-Haves

1. Candles: I love Voluspa's French Bourbon Vanille scent.

2. Red Wine: I'm Italian, so I love red wine, though I only keep organic varieties in the house since they have fewer sulfites.* My favorite is Our Daily Red, which is super-yummy and available at Whole Foods.

3. Calm Music: Bon Iver is one of my favorite artists—his music is so relaxing. And Barbra records always help me unwind.

4. Lavender Oil & Epsom Salts: If I'm tense, a few drops of Kneipp bath oil mixed in with some Epsom salts is key (it's available at Whole Foods). The Valerian & Hops always helps me fall asleep.

5. Hot Tea: If I don't feel like wine, I'll boil some water and add lemon and honey. It's a great way to rid your body of toxins. If I want flavor, I'll make Yogi's Lavender Chamomile tea.

* Sulfites keep wine from fermenting. Organic wines tend to have fewer sulfites, and dry reds have fewer than sweet whites.

The Spotlight

1. Making an effort to do something nice for yourself at the end of a long day will always make you feel better—both in that moment and the next morning. Treat yourself: Pour a glass of champagne, turn on Bravo, and slather on that masque! To me, that sounds like the greatest night ever.

2. Creating at-home pampering rituals is a great financial option. There's absolutely no reason why you can't re-create a spa experience in your own home and make it a weekly indulgence.

3. There's a major organic movement happening in skin care, which is great—and there's no better way to experiment with the concept than in your own kitchen with ingredients that are readily available from the grocery store.

4. Creating a routine is key: Don't count on an occasional facial to solve skin woes. Taking care of yourself doesn't stop when you get home—most of the work needs to happen with your own hands. Keep it up: Wash your face every morning and night, and don't pick!

5. Stay consistent. Once you find the products that work, keep them on hand and take a travel kit with you when you go. Don't throw your skin off by switching it up (and it's not just your face that counts, since even different shampoos and conditioners can have a negative effect on your hair and forehead).

FOR THE LOVE OF FOOD

"I'm a bagel on a plate full of onion rolls!"

—FANNY BRICE, *FUNNY GIRL*

My mother always taught me to respect my body—that you're only given one and should take the best care of it that you can. I've really listened to her: I never treat my body like a garbage disposal and instead try to feed it only the best possible food. After all, the right fuel is the source of the energy I need to do my job well. This has always helped me avoid falling into bad habits. I never had fast food as a kid—instead, like any traditional Italian family, we cooked all of our meals together. Food was the central theme of our lives: We showed our love over a bowl of baked ziti. So many of my favorite memories growing up took place at the family dinner table. It's there that I also learned that food could be wholesome *and* delicious and an opportunity for celebration. Quite simply, I love food: Ask my friends and they'll tell you that I'm the person who wants to talk about all the things I ate today, where we're going to dinner, and all the things we could order and eat. I really love food.

Since it's what keeps me going and makes me feel good, I've always worked hard to put it in a good perspective. Clearly, it's important to find moderation, and with moderation most certainly comes the occasional indulgence. There are definitely days when I need to eat an entire Amy's frozen pizza in front of the television. Because I generally maintain a good balance throughout the week, I never give myself a hard time about these moments. In fact, I usually turn Saturday or Sunday into a cheat day, and I *love* those days. Because it's a treat and not the norm, I truly enjoy it. It feels far more special than if I were indulging every day.

I also think this is why I've never had a crisis with food and my weight: I've never treated it like medicine for all that ails me emotionally, nor do I treat mealtime like my mortal enemy. I went to high school with a lot of girls who unfortunately had issues with food and struggled with eating disorders. Not only is it easy to take calorie counting too far, but there are way too many pressures in this world about what you should and shouldn't look like. While I completely understand why girls think they need to alter their appearance to fit in, it's so important to hold on tight to a healthy balance and love yourself by feeding your body delicious and wholesome things. Plus, looking like everyone else would be the worst thing you could do to yourself! What I was taught—and what I've learned—is that you have to really love yourself, perceived "imperfections" and all, in order to look and feel your best.

While I completely understand why girls think they need to alter their appearance to fit in, it's so important to hold on tight to a healthy balance and love yourself by feeding your body delicious and wholesome things.

And that begins with nourishing yourself with things that are good for you.

Being raised Italian, my life has always centered around dairy; I've never been into sweets. If given a choice, I'd always pick a side of macaroni and cheese for dessert over a chocolate soufflé. And for that reason, dairy and carbohydrates were the foundation of my diet before I moved to Los Angeles. When I relocated, I read a book called *Skinny Bitch,* which has a deceptive title. It's not about being skinny, it's about the truth behind all the things we eat. Up until that point, I thought a bagel in the morning, a turkey and cheese sandwich for lunch, and a bowl of pasta for dinner was the basis for a well-rounded diet. Did I mention that I love carbs? From that book, not only did I learn a lot of things about the meat industry that completely changed how I think about food, but I also learned about the importance of greens. You don't see the color green in New York a lot. After I read that book, I changed my diet completely and have totally fallen in love with fresh produce. I genuinely crave fresh salads, fresh vegetables, and fresh fruit.

Being vegetarian is my personal preference, but I've never felt like that's the sort of thing you should push on other people. I switch between being vegetarian, vegan, and pescetarian. And while I don't like eating meat now, that doesn't mean I can't change my mind someday. What will never change is that I will always give my body the fuel it needs so that I can look and feel my absolute best.

VITAMINS

I load up on as many vitamins as I can in my daily diet, but just to be sure that I'm getting enough, I visit a doctor for a B_{12} drip every week (it's a big L.A. thing). In addition, my mom gave me a Vitamix as a gift, and I supplement my meals whenever possible with freshly made juice. Thankfully, when I don't have time to make it myself, there are loads of great pressed-juice bars throughout the city. You should experiment with your favorite flavors and add more or less of each ingredient depending on your taste, but here are a few of my favorite recipes:

For a great energy boost, I'll blend three leaves of kale (de-stemmed and torn or chopped), one handful of spinach, four pieces of celery, the juice of two lemons, and a chopped-up apple. Advanced juicers tend to cut out the apple and add a few leaves of romaine or a handful of parsley instead.

For a meal supplement, I'll blend one banana with half an avocado and a handful of blueberries.

For debloating, I'll blend a glass of water with the juice of two whole lemons, half a cucumber, four to six cubes of watermelon, and a few shavings of fresh ginger.

The Eleven Snacks I Always Have on Hand

I always pack my own lunch for work (the craft services table is packed with naughty, naughty things), and I take food when I travel, too. Here's what I stash in my fridge, in my trailer on set, and in my carry-on bag, to ensure that I'm never stuck and starving.

1. Grapes

2. Seaweed

3. Kale chips (see opposite for an easy recipe, though you can buy these at the store)

4. Tzatziki (see page 74 for a modified recipe, though you can buy this at the store)

5. Carrots

6. Celery

7. Hummus

8. Luna Bars

9. Chocolate-covered goji berries

10. Cucumbers

11. Barbara's Cheese Puffs

READING A MENU

While I try to cook as much as possible, I also love to try new restaurants. Plus, I work so much that dinners out are my way of doing something social and catching up with friends. I always study the menu online in advance: I'll find a good, healthy choice, and maybe a treat, too. When I don't take a look before I sit down, I tend to order more because everything looks so exciting that I want to try it all. If I take the time to really think about what I want, and what my body needs, I don't tend to go so overboard.

Kale Chips

1 bunch of kale
Olive oil in a spray bottle
Pinch of sea salt

1. Preheat the oven to 350°F.

2. Wash and rinse the kale, and then de-stem the leaves with a small knife.

3. Tear the leaves into small bite-size chunks.

4. Place the kale on a baking sheet and spray lightly with olive oil.

5. Sprinkle the sea salt across the top.

6. Bake the kale for 10 to 15 minutes, shaking the tray every few minutes to ensure that the chips bake evenly.

KEEPING IT UP WHEN TRAVELING

When I'm on the road, I don't give myself a hard time about sticking to my normal weekly eating routine. Being that I wasn't raised on fast food, I don't see Burger King in the airport and start salivating (though if In-N-Out Burger makes its way across the country, I'll be in trouble)—so I'm never too concerned that I'll go completely off the rails.

Before I head to the airport, I always pack a lunch—I never eat plane food. It takes about two minutes to put something together in the morning, and it's usually vastly better than anything you're going to get served up in the air. Besides, I always find that I'm *most* hungry when I'm en route, so I pack a huge lunch with plenty of snacks—and get lots of jealous looks from my seatmates.

If I'm ever in a pinch, I'll find a Subway and order a whole wheat, six-inch sandwich loaded with veggies, olive oil, and a dash of vinegar.

MY FAVORITE INDULGENCES

Because you can't be good all the time!

1. In-N-Out grilled cheese sandwiches (particularly when I'm traveling)
2. Annie's macaroni and cheese
3. Amy's pizza
4. New York bagels with cream cheese, lettuce, and cucumbers
5. Bread baskets
6. Cheese plates (I love Manchego and Brie in particular)
7. Wine

WHAT I EAT IN AN AVERAGE DAY

On non-cheat days I try to keep my diet fairly simple and really make sure that what I eat is not only satisfying and delicious, but nutritious enough to give me the energy I need to do my job. Over the years, I've assembled lots of go-to meal ideas from my family, from my friends, from cookbooks, or just by experimenting in the kitchen, which I've tweaked to my taste. Here's a look at what I'm likely to eat on any given day.

DAY 1
BREAKFAST

Goat's-Milk Yogurt + Granola + Berries

1 cup goat's-milk yogurt (this is my preference, though this works with regular or Greek yogurt, too)

½ cup granola

¼ cup chopped strawberries

¼ cup blackberries

¼ cup blueberries

Top the yogurt with the granola and berries and serve!

Kale Salad + Tzatziki + Whole Wheat Toast

I like things nice and tart, which is why I usually whip up a quick red wine vinaigrette; when I'm feeling super-healthy, instead of a more traditional dressing, I'll swap in plain apple cider vinegar with some lemon and sea salt. Or I'll blend store-bought creamy miso dressing with apple cider vinegar. If you're new to kale salad, give yourself a chance to like it, and start with a thicker dressing, like an organic Caesar, before you take it in a healthier direction.

Kale Salad

1. Wash, rinse, and de-stem the kale.

2. Tear the kale into bite-size pieces.

3. Put it in a bowl with the sea salt and lemon juice, and then literally massage the pieces for about 5 minutes (or even longer).

4. When it's softened, add the olive oil.

5. Add the apple and the celery and toss to combine.

3 kale leaves

Pinch of sea salt

Juice of 1 lemon

1 teaspoon olive oil

1 apple, chopped

3 celery stalks, sliced

NOTE: Kale is a very tough green, and you really need to take your fingertips and massage and soften it to improve the taste; it sounds crazy, but it makes it much more enjoyable to eat. If you think you don't like kale, try this before you give it up entirely!

continues...

Red Wine Vinaigrette

This makes plenty for several salads, so you can store whatever's left over in a glass jar. The dressing will separate in the fridge, so give it time to come back to room temperature before you whisk it again.

....

Combine the ingredients in a bowl and whisk together.

1 teaspoon kosher salt

1 teaspoon Dijon mustard

1 garlic clove, finely chopped

3 tablespoons red wine vinegar

6 tablespoons olive oil

4 scallions, white parts thinly sliced

Tzatziki

This isn't the most "authentic" tzatziki recipe, but it's quick and delicious and makes Greek yogurt a little more exciting. This makes enough for just me, but if I have friends over, I'll multiply the recipe.

....

1. Combine all the ingredients except the lemon juice in a bowl.

2. Add the lemon juice to the mixture, stir, and serve!

1 7-ounce container Greek yogurt

1 small cucumber, peeled and cubed

1 teaspoon kosher salt

1 tablespoon apple cider vinegar

1 teaspoon olive oil

½ teaspoon minced garlic

1 tablespoon fresh dill (I love dill, use less if you don't)

Pinch of black pepper

Juice of 2 lemons

Shaved Radicchio, Parmesan, and Truffle Whole Wheat Pizza with a Sunny-Side-Up Egg + Quinoa Pasta with Marinara

I saw a variation of this pizza recipe in my friend Alicia Silverstone's excellent guide to veganism, *The Kind Diet*—my version is a little less healthy. I use store-bought whole wheat pizza shells—make sure that you check the packaging of your crust to see if it needs to be cooked a bit before you add the toppings.

continues...

Shaved Radicchio, Parmesan, and Truffle Whole Wheat Pizza with a Sunny-Side-Up Egg

1. Preheat the oven to 400°F.

2. Cook the pizza dough as the directions dictate.

3. Place the radicchio in a Ziploc bag with the lemon juice, kosher salt, and 2 tablespoons of the olive oil, and shake until it's well mixed.

4. Layer the top of the premade pizza crust with the radicchio mixture and bake until it gets crispy (you can also put it on an outdoor grill). This should take about 10 minutes.

5. Shave Parmesan cheese over the top until the pizza is covered, and continue to bake until the cheese melts, about 2 minutes.

6. Heat the remaining 1 teaspoon olive oil in a skillet over medium heat.

7. When the pan is hot, break the egg into the skillet and cook for 2 minutes.

8. When the pizza is almost finished (the radicchio will be getting crispy at this point), use a spatula to add the sunny-side-up egg (the yolk should be a bit runny) to the top of the pizza and bake for 2 minutes more.

9. If you like, add a drizzle of truffle oil over top before serving.

1 12-inch premade whole wheat pizza shell

1 head radicchio, finely shaved (if it's a large head, use half; I shave mine with a mandoline, but be careful not to cut your fingers!)

2 tablespoons fresh lemon juice

1 teaspoon kosher salt

2 tablespoons plus 1 teaspoon olive oil

Parmesan cheese

1 egg

1 teaspoon truffle oil (optional)

Quinoa Pasta + Marinara

1. Set a large pot over medium-high heat.

2. Add the olive oil to the heated pot.

3. Add the onion and garlic and cook until the onion is slightly translucent, about 5 minutes.

4. Add the tomatoes and lower the heat to medium. Season with salt to taste.

5. Cook for about an hour, stirring occasionally and pressing the tomatoes up against the side of the pan to crush them. When ready, the sauce should have a nice, thick consistency.

6. Meanwhile, boil water for the pasta with 1 tablespoon of kosher salt.

7. Cook the pasta according to the directions on the package for al dente doneness; drain and transfer to a serving bowl or platter.

8. Pour the sauce over the pasta and top with Parmesan cheese before serving.

3 tablespoons olive oil

½ onion, chopped

4 garlic cloves, minced

2 cans whole peeled tomatoes (I use San Marzano)

Kosher salt

1 pound quinoa pasta

Parmesan cheese, freshly grated

Tofu Scramble + Ezekiel Toast

....

1. Set a pan on over medium heat and let it warm.

2. Mash the tofu roughly with a fork and add it to the pan.

3. Add the salt, pepper, and cheese, and stir with a spatula.

4. Heat for about 3 minutes, or until the cheese is melted.

5. Layer the mixture over the Ezekiel toast, and top with the salsa and avocado.

1 2 x 4-inch slab firm tofu

½ teaspoon salt (or to taste)

½ teaspoon black pepper (or to taste)

2 slices rice cheese

2 pieces Ezekiel toast

2 tablespoons salsa

¼ avocado, sliced

Veggie Wrap

This is a very fast and nutritious option for a busy day—I always have these staples in my fridge for a quick power lunch.

....

1. Spread the hummus on the spinach tortilla and add the arugula, peppers, celery, and cilantro.

2. Squeeze the lemon across the mixture, sprinkle the salt over top, and roll up the tortilla.

¼ cup hummus

1 spinach tortilla

1 cup arugula

¼ red bell pepper, sliced

¼ orange bell pepper, sliced

¼ yellow bell pepper, sliced

1 celery stalk, sliced

¼ cup fresh cilantro leaves, torn

½ lemon

1 teaspoon salt

When I want to be super-healthy, I use a collard leaf instead of the spinach tortilla.

French-Style Lentil Soup

I love to top a simple but hearty lentil soup with a layer of melted Gruyère cheese—it's my own spin on French onion soup!

1. Set a stockpot over medium-high heat and add the olive oil.

2. Add the onion and sauté until translucent, about 5 minutes.

3. Add the carrots and celery and sauté for 2 minutes.

4. Stir in the lentils and sauté for 1 minute.

5. Add the vegetable stock (you can swap in water if you like your soup to taste less rich), bring the mixture to a boil, and then reduce the heat to low.

6. Let simmer for 30 minutes.

7. Preheat the oven to 200°F.

8. Season with salt and pepper to taste.

9. Ladle the soup into an oven-safe bowl, add the cheese, and pop into the oven until the cheese is melted, about 2 minutes.

2 tablespoons olive oil

1 onion, finely chopped

2 carrots, diced

2 celery stalks, diced

1 cup canned lentils, rinsed

6 cups vegetable stock

Salt

Black pepper

¼ cup grated Gruyère

Egg White Frittata

....

1. Preheat the oven to 375°F.

2. Heat the olive oil in a heavy oven-safe skillet over medium-low heat.

3. Add the bell peppers and onion and sauté until tender, about 7 minutes.

4. Sprinkle the mixture with the salt and black pepper.

5. Pour the egg whites into the skillet and cook for 3 minutes.

6. Sprinkle the feta and spinach over top.

7. Put the skillet in the oven and bake, uncovered, for 8 to 10 minutes.

8. Loosen the edges of the frittata with a rubber spatula and then invert onto a plate.

2 tablespoons olive oil

1 red bell pepper, seeded and chopped

1 green bell pepper, seeded and chopped

¼ onion, chopped

1 teaspoon kosher salt

1 teaspoon black pepper

8 egg whites (you can separate eggs or buy egg whites in a carton)

½ cup crumbled feta cheese

8 ounces fresh spinach

Veggie Lentil Burger

1. Bring 2½ cups salted water to a boil. Add the lentils and cook for 45 minutes.

2. Preheat the oven to 200°F. Line a baking sheet with parchment paper.

3. In a saucepan, heat the olive oil. Add the onion and carrot and sauté until tender, about 5 minutes.

4. In a large bowl, combine the onion, carrot, lentils, pepper, soy sauce, bread crumbs, and egg.

5. Form the mixture into patties and place them on the lined baking sheet.

6. Bake the burgers for 20 to 25 minutes. Place them on a dish or serving platter.

7. In the same pan you used for the onion and carrot, wilt the spinach, about 2 minutes.

8. Squeeze the lemon over the spinach and spoon it over the burgers.

9. Top the burgers with anything else that you like—I usually add a slice of vegan pepper Jack cheese, some organic ketchup, and a few slices of avocado. Serve on a whole grain bun, if you like.

1 cup dry lentils, picked over and rinsed

½ onion, finely chopped

½ carrot, finely chopped

2 tablespoons olive oil

Black pepper

1 tablespoon soy sauce

¾ cup bread crumbs

1 egg

½ cup spinach

½ lemon

OPTIONAL TOPPINGS

1 slice vegan pepper Jack cheese

Organic ketchup

¼ avocado, sliced

1 whole grain burger bun

DINNER

Salmon + Asparagus

I always buy wild Alaskan salmon—when it's high-quality, it tastes great with the simplest of preparations.

....

1. Start a grill and let it heat until it's dry and hot.

2. Put the rice in a rice cooker; if you don't have a rice cooker, you can use the stovetop (follow the directions on the package, though in general it's a ratio of 1:2 of rice to water).

3. Brush the salmon with 1 teaspoon of the olive oil, sprinkle the pink side with a bit of sea salt, and pour the lemon juice on top.

4. Place the salmon on the grill, skin side down, and cook for 8 to 10 minutes.

5. Drizzle the asparagus with the remaining 1 teaspoon olive oil and some sea salt, and carefully place each spear on the grill.

6. Flip the salmon flesh side down and grill for a few minutes, until cooked to your liking.

7. Once the asparagus are nicely charred and tender, about 5 minutes, remove from the heat and serve them alongside the salmon and rice.

1   cup uncooked brown rice

    Half a salmon fillet

2   teaspoons olive oil

    Sea salt

    Juice of 1 lemon

6   asparagus spears

NAVIGATING THE GROCERY STORE

I'm a strong believer in keeping my house healthy. Some of it's *really* healthy, like gluten-free bread and rice cheese, and some of it is a little naughty (but never terrible). That way, when I do feel like indulging, I have good choices. I save major treat time for when I go out with friends.

I love going to the grocery store. It's dorky, but it's part of my perfect day. I put on my headphones, listen to great music, and really take my time to shop. This gives me the chance to really look and check out the options, which is how I happened upon most of my favorite healthy alternatives. I only found Ezekiel bread (a low-glycemic "live" bread that's healthy, delicious, and packed with grains like lentils and barley) because I stopped to linger in the bread aisle to weigh my options; same with Redwood Hill goats-milk yogurt, which has probiotics, vitamins, minerals, and complete proteins. It's so easy to go straight for the things we know and love—but there might be something right next to your go-to that you'll love even more. Give yourself plenty of time to read labels, check things out, and hopefully take some chances!

CHECK THE GROCERY STORE FOR HEALTHIER ALTERNATIVES TO YOUR FAVORITE FOODS.

The Spotlight

1. Remember that your body is your temple. It deserves good things to eat that will give you the energy and strength you need to take on your day.

2. Resist the urge to count calories. You can consume all of your calories through Hershey's Kisses and not give your body the nutrition it really needs; alternately, starving yourself isn't an option, either.

3. When you're going out for dinner, read the menu in advance so you can be thoughtful about your choices.

4. Check the grocery store for healthier alternatives to your favorite foods—you might be surprised that there's an even yummier (healthy) version of Cheetos.

5. Pack a lunch when you're traveling—not only is it far more nutritious (airplane meals tend to have a ton of sodium, too), but you'll never go hungry looking for the peanut cart.

→ In action at the grocery store.

LIVING THE FIT LIFE

"I'm a work in progress."
— BARBRA STREISAND

Needless to say, acting—particularly on a show like *Glee* requires a lot of energy. Actually, scratch that: Life in general requires a lot of energy. I can't roll onto set out of shape or sleep-deprived and summon everything I need to make Rachel Berry come alive on the screen. Besides wanting to feel generally *good*, one of the requirements of my job is that I really bring it to the set.

When I lived in New York, I never belonged to a gym, or even gave a second thought to scheduling in exercise, because, plain and simple, I was constantly on the move. On Broadway, I spent my days dancing numbers on the stage, which is arguably equal to about three spin classes. And even during my days off, I wasn't sitting around. Walking the New York City streets and heading up and down the subway steps is a workout; it's easy to put in the miles without even thinking about it. Because of this, I got a little spoiled.

Thanks to my Italian heritage, it's safe to say that I love carbs. When I was on Broadway, I was easily burning more calories than I consumed without any extra effort, so if I ate a box of Annie's organic macaroni and cheese when I got home from doing two shows, I really didn't think much of it. Thanks to my anti-sedentary lifestyle, though, I had plenty of energy to perform—and then some. But when I moved to Los Angeles, things changed.

Los Angeles is a car culture, and because you drive everywhere, you're automatically sitting around for most of the day (hello, traffic!). I didn't really take this into account when I relocated; in fact, because L.A. has some of the best produce around, and you get to be outside 365 days a year, I figured I'd be my healthiest yet! Not so much. After the first few months of filming, I started to feel a bit tired and listless, and giving Rachel the vivaciousness she requires and deserves was becoming a struggle. I've never owned a scale, and the costume department never made a point of it, but when the season aired, and I got to see myself on TV, it was clear that I had gained about five or six pounds between episode 2 and episode 12. Five or six pounds may not sound like a lot, but when you're five foot two, it's very visible!

I really didn't care that I had gained weight—I cared that I didn't feel well and didn't have as much energy as I really needed to play Rachel every day. For that, I needed all the help I could get! I had already sworn off late-night meals from the craft services truck (rice and pan-fried vegetables, yum!) and started to inject a lot more movement into my days. On Broadway, I was doing eight shows a week involving a lot of dancing. While *Glee* is active, the schedule is different every day: Sometimes we're doing musical numbers and learning choreography for hours on end—and then there are the days that we're sitting in the choir room. And sitting is all we do.

I started to investigate all my workout options, which was a whole new world to me. And because

working out sucks sometimes, I wanted to try to make it as fun as possible and try everything until I found the best fit. There are a handful of different exercise tribes in Los Angeles: There are the gym rats, who spend hours at Equinox or the famous Venice-based Gold's Gym doing a majority of their socializing, people-watching, and mirror-gazing; there are the studio addicts, who are exclusively devoted to SoulCycle, Tracy Anderson, or Pop Physique; and then there are those who take advantage of L.A.'s preternaturally nice year-round weather and spend their downtime biking along the Pacific Coast Highway or hiking in Mandeville Canyon. After a lot of trial and error, I determined that I belong to the last two tribes: I have the luxury of enlisting an amazing trainer, Devon Butler, who helps me make the most of my own backyard for various strength-training exercises, and then I spend my weekends exploring L.A.'s hiking trails and popping into the occasional class.

I really urge you to try everything, because the right experience can completely change your perspective on exercise and make you actually look forward to moving around. When I started the class circuit, I was initially intimidated to try a spin class, since everyone told me they were so hard. But I discovered that I loved spinning—and what's even better, I was actually good at it! And same with Bikram yoga: I'd only heard horror stories and been told that I'd hate it, but I actually love stretching it out in such a hot room. Meanwhile, I thought I would love Pilates but found it's not for me. So, I've found that the combination of hiking, yoga, and working out in my backyard makes me the happiest—with an occasional spin class with a friend thrown in for good measure. Scheduling workouts well in advance really helps me stick to them, and I ask friends to text me when they're going to a class in case I can join, because having company is an extra incentive (also, you feel extra bad when you bail!).

The reason I love working out in my backyard with Devon is that I can keep it extremely focused—and she makes it so much fun for me, which is the real trick of it all. If you find classes, a routine, or workout buddies that make this a time you can actually look forward to, it's so much easier to push through a challenging hour. I can accomplish everything there that I would in a gym (without the gym fees or the travel time). I know trainers are really expensive, so that's why Devon and I have included my favorite exercises in this chapter, which you can do in your own home with just a few tools. (I often do them on my own, though Devon pushes me harder than I can push myself!) In a good week, I try to work out three times: Devon and I will do one session in my backyard, and then we schedule in one hike and one yoga session. Finding local hiking trails and exploring your city by foot is a great way to experience your area and get your heart rate up—all without spending a dime.

When it comes to fitness, it's most important to take your own internal temperature and see how you feel: Feeling listless? As counterintuitive as

Finding local hiking trails and exploring your city by foot is a great way to experience your area and get your heart rate up—all without spending a dime.

it may be, a vigorous walk will inject so much energy into the rest of your day. It doesn't really matter how often you work out or how many reps you get in; what matters most is that you're listening to your body and giving it what it needs. It can be so hard to motivate to get up and moving—so hard!—but you'll always feel better afterward. Now, of course, I always feel better after sitting on my couch and watching an episode of *Don't Be Tardy* on Bravo. Some days, that *is* what your body needs—and if I've been diligent about getting my exercise in, I'll always cut myself some slack and couch potato it out. But if it's been a few days, I try to do something small: A quick walk on the treadmill is enough to get me restarted and reenergized, and ultimately back on track.

SWEAT ESSENTIALS

*Devon's Five Quick Ways
To Add More Movement
To Your Life*

1. Always take the stairs instead of the elevator.
2. When you go to the mall or the grocery store, aim for the parking spot as far from the entrance as possible—then do biceps curls with your groceries or shopping bags as you walk back.
3. Do squats or sit-ups during commercial breaks.
4. If you have a pet or a child, get down on the floor and play.
5. Instead of using a traditional desk chair, swap it for a stability ball—this forces you to work on your posture and your abs during computer time.

I bought a bike so that I could ride it around the Paramount lot between takes!

I tried snowboarding and it was a crazy-good workout—I incorporate activities into as much of my free time as possible.

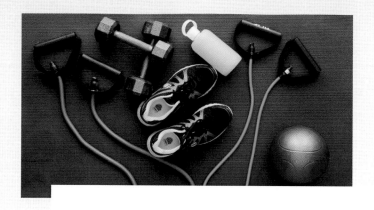

Motivation Mix/Sweat Mix

1. "Sexy Back"—Justin Timberlake
2. "Locked Out of Heaven"—Bruno Mars
3. "I Love It"—Icona Pop
4. "Womanizer"—Britney Spears
5. "Run the World (Girls)"—Beyoncé
6. "Starships"—Nicki Minaj
7. "Americano/Dance Again"—Glee
8. "Firework"—Katy Perry
9. "Dancing on My Own"
    —Robyn
10. "Only Girl (in the World)"
    —Rihanna

WORKING OUT THE KINKS

There's nothing worse than a big, painful knot in your back—it can make it hard to work, to relax, and even to sleep. When stretching isn't enough, you often need immediate relief—without necessarily breaking the bank on an expensive spa massage. Big knots require intense pressure (more than a helpful friend can provide), so I use my own body weight and a tennis ball to really work out the kinks. You lie on a tennis ball and position it under your knot. You can move around a bit until the knot is gone!

WORKING OUT IN YOUR OWN BACKYARD

This is how Devon keeps me red-carpet ready—you can do these exercises with minimal equipment in your own backyard!

Dynamic Stretch Warm-Up

It is important to warm up with dynamic stretches, which involve moving through the muscles in the stretched position. Static stretching (think old-school gym-class stretches) should be done at the end of the workout, as it forces the muscles to relax and ultimately turns them off. While this is perfect as a cool-down, it's not the right tactic at the beginning of a workout—in contrast, dynamic stretches prepare the muscles for weight-bearing activity.

Beautiful baby Juliette was born in 2013!

1 DYNAMIC LEG SWINGS – 15 EACH SIDE

This is a dynamic stretch to get the entire system warmed up. Straighten your leg and swing it forward, and then bend it as you swing it back. Increase your range of motion as your muscles stretch and warm up. This stretches the quad, hamstring, and psoas (hip flexor).

2 DYNAMIC ARM SWINGS— 20 SWINGS TOTAL

Swing your arms back at shoulder level, stretching through your pecs and shoulders.

Then swing your arms forward so they wrap around you and touch opposite parts of the back. This stretches the shoulders, biceps, pecs, and upper back.

3 ALTERNATING SQUATS— 60 SECONDS

Start with your feet together, step to the right, and do a squat. Then step your feet back together, step out to the left, and squat. Keep alternating the legs, doing as many as you can over the course of a minute. This gently warms up the body and gets the heart rate slightly elevated.

WORKOUT CIRCUIT
(REPEAT THREE TIMES)

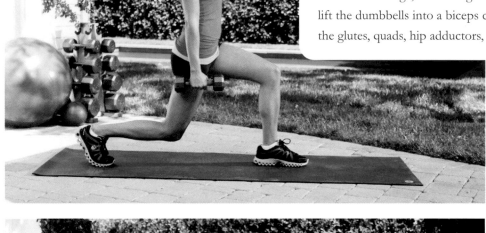

1 STATIONARY LUNGE/BICEPS CURL – 15 REPS EACH SIDE

Place your legs in a deep lunge position (one leg in front of the other) so that both knees can get to a ninety-degree angle when bent, and hold a five- to eight-pound dumbbell loosely in each hand at your sides. Bend your knees and drop down into a lunge, then straighten your legs and lift the dumbbells into a biceps curl. This targets the glutes, quads, hip adductors, and biceps.

2 FULL PLANK WITH TWIST – ALTERNATING, 20 REPS ON EACH SIDE

Hold a full plank (the top of a push-up position), with your feet as wide apart as your hands. Bend one knee and twist to touch it to the opposite elbow, keeping your abs engaged and hips lifted to shoulder level (so your lower back does not sag). This targets the obliques, shoulders, and abs.

3 JUMPING JACKS WITH SHOULDER PRESSES— 60 SECONDS

Jump your feet out and in, in a traditional jumping-jack fashion, while lifting your arms (with a three-pound dumbbell in each hand) straight overhead from a shoulder-press position every time your legs go wide. This targets the legs and shoulders.

4 SQUAT/ROW—20 REPS

Take a resistance band and wrap it around something very sturdy at shoulder level (ideally, use a door frame attachment). Hold the handles and move back until the band is taut. Reach your arms forward as you drop your hips back and bend your knees into a squat (you should look as though you're sitting in a chair, and your knees should never go forward beyond your toes). As you straighten your legs to stand, pull the handles back to your rib cage and squeeze your shoulder blades together. This targets the glutes, core, and upper back.

5 KICKBACKS (MODIFIED BURPEE)—15 REPS

Start in a standing position and then descend into a squat. Place your hands in front of your feet and jump back to a plank, then jump back to a squat (keep your back flat) and return to standing. This targets the full body and is good cardio.

6 SUPINE REVERSE CRUNCH—25 REPS

Lie on your back on a mat with your arms behind your head in a traditional sit-up position. Lift your shoulder blades high off the ground so that your abs are engaged. Bring your bent knees in to touch your elbows, then kick your legs out straight at 45 degrees (or lower, as you get stronger), and then pull them back in to your elbows using your lower abs. Make sure that you keep your back pressed against the mat so that it doesn't arch. If it does, kick your legs out at a higher angle. This targets the upper and lower abs.

COOL DOWN
(REPEAT ON BOTH SIDES)

1 HAMSTRING STRETCH— HOLD FOR 30 SECONDS

Lie on your back on a mat and lift your right leg straight up toward the sky. Depending on your flexibility, grab either at the ankle or behind the knee and pull your leg in toward your face. You can also use a towel or yoga strap to wrap around your foot.

2 HIP STRETCH— HOLD FOR 30 SECONDS

While lying on your back, cross your right ankle over your bent left knee and place both hands behind your left hamstring. Pull your legs in toward your chest.

3 LOWER-BACK STRETCH— HOLD FOR 30 SECONDS

While still on your back, keep your right knee bent, and then twist your right leg across your body so that your right knee ends up next to your left hip. Stretch your arms straight out to your sides, and look over your right shoulder.

The Spotlight

1. Try as many exercise options as possible to figure out what works best for you. After all, it's an amazing feeling to find a routine that you love and actually look forward to doing. Find a great physical activity that can be your golden ticket to a fit life and requires minimal motivation to do. Keep an open mind: You might have the most fun in a Broadway show-tunes-themed spin class or an eighties aerobic session! You never know!

2. Figure out what you're trying to achieve, whether it's an increase of energy, general detox, weight loss, weight gain, or a spiritual experience. If you want to lose weight, buy a Jillian Michaels DVD and have her yell at you; if you're looking to unwind, that may not be the best solution.

3. Know when you're slacking off, and don't fool yourself into thinking that it doesn't matter—try to just do *something* to get yourself moving. That said, when you need a break, take one! Taking a day off is an important part of being good to yourself, too. If you do skip the gym, then enjoy the moment and don't feel guilty or

beat yourself up about it; that can quickly make exercise feel like a chore and cause you to obsess (and avoid the gym even more). View your workouts as a treat and something positive to look forward to.

4. Take some time on Sunday to schedule your upcoming week of exercise: When it's in your calendar, it's easier to mentally prepare for your workout. Don't trust yourself to decide in the moment whether you're going to go to the gym or not; it's too easy to take a pass. Just make it a given.

5. Find a workout buddy: If you have consistent plans to meet a friend for a weekly hike or a gym class, you're much less likely to flake.

EVERYDAY STYLE

"I go by instinct—I don't worry about experience."
—BARBRA STREISAND

When I was in *Ragtime*, a fellow cast member named Monica told me that fabulous is twenty-four hours a day, and it stuck. In fact, you can laugh, but I'm the girl who wears nightgowns to bed. True story: I love falling asleep wearing something pretty—or at the very least, something matching, even if it's just a black T-shirt and black shorts. I don't wear oversize T-shirts, and I don't wear things that have holes. Ever. And I have to say, making an effort makes me feel amazing.

These days, I often have four a.m. call times, and it is oh-so-tempting to roll onto set in yoga pants and an oversize hoodie. But I made a New Year's resolution that my job is my job, and that I should show it the proper respect by putting on a real outfit in the morning. To make it happen, I've reverted to a tactic I used in high school that may sound crazy but actually saves me tons of time. I literally plot out a week's worth of outfits so that I can reach for them when I'm groggy in the early morning and don't have to spend any extra minutes in front of my closet, trying to put something together. It doesn't mean that I'm in high heels, it just means that I'm dressed appropriately for my job. I may have "made it" in some sense of the term, but that doesn't mean I've given up or ever want to take things for granted. I always want to represent myself well.

During every magazine interview, I always get asked how I would describe my personal style. And it's very clear that everyone who asks is always bored by my answer: My personal style is quite simple. I'm a "jeans and T-shirt" kind of girl, and prefer to express my more creative side at work, in photo shoots, or on the red carpet. In my everyday life, I don't dress in knee-high stockings and penny loafers à la Rachel Berry, nor do I ever wear gowns when I'm not at a big event. My basic concern is that I look nice and pulled together whenever I leave the house.

The pieces I rely on to help me look nice and pulled together generally aren't huge splurges, either. Whenever I'm interviewed, I also always get asked about my last big purchase. But quite honestly, I don't spend a lot when I shop: I buy really well-made things that are going to last, and only a few things at that. I've always been more interested in quality than quantity. I don't believe that girls need to own eight thousand pairs of shoes and six thousand bags: I'll usually invest in one nice bag per year. If something is great, I try to get great use out of it—and it's hard to get great use out of anything when it only makes it out of your closet once every two months!

FAVORITE OUTFIT AS A KID

When I was little, my main look was black leggings, a long-sleeve T-shirt, white socks rolled up over the leggings, and flats. So, no . . . I didn't have great fashion sense. I grew up in a wealthy community in New Jersey where status was key:

What you wore to school was of utmost importance. Since I came from a family that was less wealthy—not in the real world, but definitely in a town where people lived in mansions and sixth-grade girls used Prada bags as pencil cases—I wasn't allowed to splurge on the $100 jeans my friends wore. And my parents were right to set those limits. I'm so glad I didn't get to buy whatever I wanted, because I learned to really value what I did own. And I also learned that you don't need to have what everyone else has to fit in.

MOST IMPORTANT PIECE

My grandfather bought me a necklace before he passed away that I'll always cherish. It's a small diamond necklace, and I love it so much. I'll also always keep Rachel's finn necklace from *Glee*.

STYLE ICON

I really love Rachel Bilson's style, because she always seems to get it right without trying too hard. I loved her as Summer on *The O.C.*, and it's been fun to watch her develop such a great career and establish herself as a real fashion icon. Her effortless and comfortable style is how I love to dress on a typical day.

FIRST IMPORTANT PIECE

When I first got *Glee*, I bought myself a Balenciaga bag. It was the first big purchase I'd ever made. I think it's better to splurge on a great bag or a beautiful piece of jewelry than something like a dress. Accessories generally aren't part of fleeting trends and they last longer.

THE BEST THINGS I'VE EVER BOUGHT

These are the items that marked milestones in my life—and that I wore to death.

JEANS: These Citizens of Humanity skinny jeans fit me the best.

HEELS: These were a gift from Cory—I thought it was so special that he bought me shoes, since guys don't usually have the first clue about buying them.

LEATHER JACKET: I bought that at my friend's boutique, Switch, and I think it's super-badass.

BAG: This Balenciaga bag was my big splurge when I landed *Glee*.

MY STYLE ON BOTH COASTS

NEW YORK

I never realized until I moved to Los Angeles that when I lived full-time in New York, I only wore black. It's a cliché, but it's true: In New York, black tends to be everyone's uniform. But black is never boring. In fact, when I'm there I tend to a have a lot more fun with my wardrobe by layering and adding accessories—you can get away with so much more in that city when it comes to fashion. I'll still usually wear black, but I'll add a red lip, or wear a lot of accessories or fun patterned stockings (I guess that's the Rachel Berry in me). New York City just allows for more creativity: You're surrounded by a sea of interesting and eclectic people who are out walking around, plus there are changing seasons, which means layers (often cool vintage ones) are in constant play.

LOS ANGELES

Living in New York, I always fantasized about what it might be like to live on the West Coast and wear shorts, flip-flops, and T-shirts all year round. Now that I'm actually in L.A., I can confess that when I'm at home, I get to live out my dream. Los Angeles has some big-time fashion credibility, but it will always be more casual and less sartorially creative than New York—I don't know if it's because it's permanently sunny and layer resistant or because people are just not out walking around as much (it's a car culture, after all), but most people's style is much more straightforward and much more label-conscious. (There isn't as much of a thrift shop culture, either.) To that end, I find that when I'm in L.A., my style is simpler, too.

← Catching a bite to eat in New York City with my mom and dad. I love dressing up a simple pair of pants and a top with a cozy sweater and heels.

DRESSING A PETITE FRAME

This sounds a bit unintentionally raunchy, but I believe that if you're short, you need to show as much skin as possible. Stylists at photo shoots tend to want to put a lot of fabric on me, but that doesn't work when you're five foot two. (That said, I'm actually considered tall in my family . . . my mother is four foot eleven!) Too much draping makes me look even more stunted and consumes my entire frame. I need to wear baggier pants with a fitted tank top, and slouchy sweaters with shorts. And I'm always a big fan of minidresses—in fact, I often take dresses to the tailor to have them shortened even more.

The Six-Month Replenishment Plan

It's the little things that count, and nothing can undermine a day faster than poorly fitting, stretched-out socks or ratty underwear. Every six months, I make it a point to replenish my selection of both of these things and weed out the T-shirts and tank tops that have seen better days. Generally, I only buy all these essentials in white and black— sure, I've gravitated to the occasional fluorescent yellow and pink bra before, but ultimately, I like to remind myself that a clean and simple wardrobe is best. (That way, you never have to worry about not matching, either.)

Ultimately, dressing a petite frame is about balance and finding one part of your body to reveal. I love my legs and think that they're my best feature, so I love to show them off.

↑ This is a good example of how I like to show a little bit of leg while exercising some restraint up top.

MAXIMIZING MY SHOPPING BUDGET

I don't treat shopping as a sport—nor do I spend wildly and carelessly. I'm very strategic about what I buy and when I buy it to ensure that I never waste money and never add things to my closet that I'm not going to wear.

1. I ALWAYS MAKE A LIST. I shop seasonally, twice a year. That way, I know exactly what I need and try to get it all in just one or two spots. If I go out looking to shop—and not for something specific—I always waste money on things I don't need and don't ultimately wear.

2. I SHOP BY OUTFIT. Rather than picking up pieces bit by bit, I ask salespeople to help me put together outfits. I'll walk out with three complete looks, rather than ten separate pieces, and know exactly how to put it all together.

3. I PICK PIECES THAT FIT. This may sound like a no-brainer, but I never buy things that need extensive tailoring. If it doesn't more or less fit, it doesn't come home with me—small tweaks and alterations are fine, but if it's a total overhaul, it's just not worth it.

4. I FOCUS ON JUST ONE STORE. I resist the temptation to skip from shop to shop—when I stick to one comprehensive store and really focus, I always end up buying everything I need, rather than a necklace here and a dress there.

FAVORITE STORES

SWITCH, BEVERLY HILLS

When I just want to make one stop, this is my favorite place to go. In general, I don't like shopping in large stores, since they can quickly start to feel overwhelming. I can't focus in big department stores, and I won't dig through barrels at thrift stores in search of buried treasures. If it's not well edited and placed in front of my face, I won't find it. I love shopping at Switch because everything I need is there, from evening to casual, and I never waste money on things I don't end up wearing.

BARNEYS CO-OP

This is where I go when I'm ready to splurge a bit, because they have really high-quality brands, and I know everything I pick here will last a long time.

URBAN OUTFITTERS

They have the best cute, short dresses—I buy a lot of stuff there for my time in New York.

ANTHROPOLOGIE

I love Anthro's selection of nightgowns and comfortable clothing.

the Comfort of a Cozy Sweater

My mother buys me a cozy sweater every year on my birthday, and it's become one of my favorite ways to mark the passing of time. It's pretty much the best gift. After all, a really nice, well-made, comfortable sweater is not the sort of thing you'd buy for yourself.

FAVORITE BRANDS

HELMUT LANG: It's expensive but has great quality that always lasts.

VINCE: These pieces are also pricey, but they're well made and extremely comfy; I always invest in their tank tops in particular.

SWITCH: I love their house line of T-shirts.

CLOSET ORGANIZATION

In short, I'm an anti-hoarder: If I haven't worn something in the past year, then I pass it on to someone who *will* use or wear it.

If I had my druthers, I'd go to everyone's house and organize their closets for them. Nothing is a quicker path to aggravation and wasted time (and money) than an overstuffed closet. I clean mine out constantly.

I don't own a lot of things, specifically because I like to be able to clearly see all my options. Plus, I then never run the risk of buying something only to find that I have three similar items tucked away in the back corner of my wardrobe. And I also just don't have the patience or inclination to weed through a sea of dresses and tops to find something to wear.

The Spotlight

1. Closet organization is key. Not only does it help you feel more generally together, but when you're shopping it's much more budget-friendly to know exactly what you need. (And then you have to stick to your list.)

2. You don't need to own a lot of things to have a great wardrobe—and great style.

3. Find what works for you and rock it—and then exercise a little restraint. After all, didn't Coco Chanel say that before you leave your house you should take one accessory off?

4. Think of shopping as a treat rather than a habit—and be pointed in your missions so you don't aimlessly buy that sweater you're never going to wear.

5. Ask for help: If you're looking to revamp your wardrobe, find a sales associate whose style you admire or who has a similar body shape and ask her to put some outfits together for you so you don't end up with a bunch of random pieces. And as annoying as it is, try things on before you leave the store!

RED CARPET FASHION

"I arrived in Hollywood without having my nose fixed, my teeth capped, or my name changed. That is very gratifying to me."

BARBRA STREISAND

Just like with a wedding or a prom, you hope that you won't look back at photos from an important night out and cringe. You hope that you'll be able to look back and wish you could relive that moment again and again. It usually comes down to the dress, and whether it's amazing, and timeless, and the right cut for your body shape. If there's one thing that my stylist, Estee Stanley, has drilled into me over the years, it's that it isn't really about fitting into a great dress—it's about a dress working for you. After all, what's the point of wearing a gorgeous gown if you have to change yourself to make it work? Don't pick something that de-

pends on your dropping a few pounds or (impossibly) growing a couple of inches.

When I was a little girl, my mom and I would put on fancy dresses, make a cheese platter, pour glasses of nonalcoholic cider, and watch the award shows. When people would win, I would make speeches on their behalf and hold giant imaginary statues. Some girls play house, some girls play with their Easy-Bake ovens, but I was playing red carpet arrivals at the Oscars. It was pure fantasy—I never thought I'd actually attend

← In Oscar de la Renta at my first Golden Globes, when I was nominated for best actress in a comedy. This is still my favorite red carpet look (can you spot my mom in the background?).

something like that in real life. Flash forward twenty years and there I was, actually sitting at the Golden Globes with my mom, wearing Oscar de la Renta and getting nominated with the best of the best.

From day one, Estee has always let me pick the dress that made me feel the best. Every once in a while she'll push me to take a risk or try out a designer I've never worn before, but as long as the dress makes me feel beautiful, I'm game for pretty much anything. Sometimes I think Estee tests me to see if she can guess my taste. At my very first Golden Globes, Ryan Murphy didn't want us to wear black—he wanted us to look young and festive, and so Estee called in a huge rack of pastel gowns. At my fitting, I headed to the bathroom and walked through Estee's insane closet on my way, where I saw this gorgeous black Oscar de la Renta gown hanging up. I know she put it in my path to see if it would make me stop—and stop I did. It was part of her personal collection, but I knew it was the one, even though she kept reminding me that I hadn't wanted to wear black. I didn't try on anything else that day. I sent Ryan a photo and told him that while I knew he didn't want me to wear black, I had found "the One." He asked me who it was by, I told him, and he replied, "It's perfect." The fact that it was Oscar definitely overshadowed the fact that it wasn't pastel! Estee and I added some green earrings, and I was off to the red carpet, where the dress really established me as

having some style credibility. I had never thought of myself as a trendsetter or as having great personal fashion sense, but that dress helped me find my footing in the world of the red carpet, where I've been comfortable ever since. Maybe it's all that practice that I got in with my mom, but I think that when you have an A-team, and you feel good about yourself inside, you'll always look your best.

Case in point: Sometimes things happen that require you to switch it all up on the go—and not only do you need to be flexible, but you can't let it rattle you. The first year I went to the Grammys I was all set to wear this beautiful white dress. I put it on and was ready to head out the door when we realized that the tailor had messed up the lining and it was unwearable. I would be lying if I didn't say I was panicking: You prep really hard prior to a big event with fittings et al., and you have a very clear picture in your head of what you're going to look like, so having to switch it up at the last second is very scary. An unflappable Estee ran to her car to see what else she might have and came up with this one-shoulder feathery navy dress from Romona Keveza. We threw it on, it fit, and I was out the door. People loved the dress, and it got amazing press, which just goes to show that if you're comfortable with yourself and you rock it, you can make anything work. It was a great lesson for me.

➔ Fitting photos Estee and I took of the gowns before they hit the red carpet.

It probably also helped that it was a short dress, which is my go-to: I love to show off my legs, and so I always feel extra-confident when I'm playing up that part of my body. It's very important to know what flatters your frame best and to be realistic about your body (e.g., I'll never, ever be tall). I never go into fittings planning to lose five pounds to make something that doesn't quite work look great, just as I never try on gowns with my hair and makeup done. If you try on an important dress without any of the extras, and you still like how you look, then you can know that on the big day, when you're all put together, the entire effect will be next-level.

Those next-level moments are insanely fun and still feel so special. Getting ready takes me right back to those evenings with my mom when I played dress-up: It's all such a fantasy, I can barely believe it's my real life. To make your real-life moments truly magical—whether it's a school dance, your wedding, or a black-tie affair—Estee agreed to share all her red carpet tips to help you look your very best, to find the right fit for your body, and to elevate any dress with accessories. But first, we wanted to recount the stories behind some of our favorite gowns.

MY FIVE FAVORITE RED CARPET MOMENTS

1. The first year I was nominated for an Emmy, I was going through an Oscar de la Renta phase. It was one of those nights where everything worked: the blue dress, the hair, the makeup, the jewelry. I felt so pretty and landed my first *Women's Wear Daily* cover, which in the world of fashion is major.

2. As I mentioned, I felt like a princess in the black Oscar de la Renta gown I borrowed from Estee to wear to my first Golden Globes (see page 120). I couldn't believe that I could wear something so beautiful and not be considered overdressed. Instead, I completely fit in, and as I was coming from an entirely different world (Broadway), it was so important that the dress made me *feel* like I belonged. You wouldn't guess, but it was actually one of the more comfortable dresses I've ever worn. You always remember when a dress is comfortable.

3. I wore a Pucci dress to the Chrysalis Butterfly Ball in 2012, and I went with Cory. I remember being so excited for him to see me in that dress because I thought it was gorgeous, with a low back and an awesome print. Mark gave me some cool new bangs, Melanie did a fun pink lip, and it was an amazing night all around.

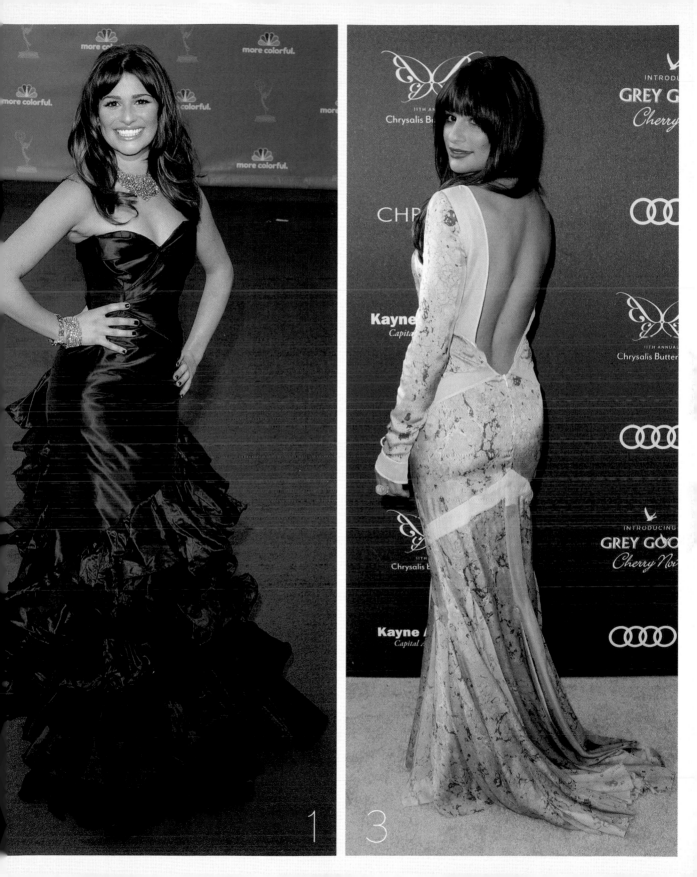

4. I wore a see-through silver Marchesa dress to the Golden Globes in 2012 that was a bit risky because it was quite revealing, but the minute I got there, I ran into Ryan, and he looked at me and said, "Love." Not only is Ryan my work hero, but I always defer to his taste—he has a deep knowledge of fashion, and so I always appreciate it when he likes what I'm wearing. This dress was a home run for me, and another example of when the dress, jewelry, hair, and makeup all worked together.

5. I loved the dress that I wore to the SAG Awards in 2012: It was Versace and it had a huge slit that featured the legs, which is rare to find. We did very simple hair and makeup and really focused on the gown, which made me feel so sexy.

4

5

THE DRESS
THAT MADE ME ILL
(ONE OF ESTEE'S PICKS)

I wore a Marchesa dress to the 2011 People's Choice Awards that was absolutely stunning: It was covered with this beautiful white flapper-style beading. I loved the hair and makeup too, because Melanie did a fabulous bright pink lip. I took my cousin as my date that night and won an award—I felt a little ill but chalked it up to nerves from the night. After, we all went to a big dinner, where I ultimately had to excuse myself because I just didn't feel good. I headed back to my house with my cousin, changed out of my dress, and instantly felt better—it was only at that moment that my cousin picked up the dress and exclaimed how heavy it was. We weighed it, and it came in at more than twenty pounds! I was literally being pulled to the ground by my dress all night!

Comfort

We've talked a lot in this chapter about how to look great at an important event, but it's equally important that you feel comfortable. Because when you're comfortable, you're relaxed, which is a key ingredient to looking your best. If you slip on a gown and feel uncomfortable in the dressing room, then you're certainly going to be uncomfortable at the end of a long post-event party. You have to be able to breathe, and you have to trust that your dress isn't going to fall down or split up the back. And you need to be able to walk without limping! Every woman loves an amazing pair of shoes, but if they're not going to be front and center, go for comfort instead. With most long dresses, nobody will ever see your heels, so there's no point in destroying your feet. It's much more elegant to be able to move around an event with ease.

WHAT WAS
I THINKING?

At the beginning of *Glee* I went to the Fox Eco-Casino Party, and I picked out my dress myself: It looked like a rock 'n' roll tutu! We did a red lip and long, black Morticia Addams extensions to match. I remember feeling confident that I looked hot, but when I look back now I cringe: too much hair, too much makeup, and a totally crazy dress. This was a perfect illustration of why it is often wise to focus on just one thing.

The Spotlight

1. Never choose a dress that requires you to change yourself; find one that truly works for you, as *you*.

2. When trying on a gown, remember that if you don't go to the dressing room all done up, you'll be able to get an idea of the dress without hair and makeup.

3. Being comfortable will make you look even more beautiful. Obviously, we all want to look amazing and big-event-worthy, but if you don't feel like you can move and hang out with ease, it's not worth it.

4. Always pick something that's timeless rather than trendy—you'll be able to look back on it in a decade and still love how you looked.

5. Try to block out the noise when your friends are telling you that something looks great when it doesn't feel right. You are the most important judge.

ESTEE STANLEY'S TEN RED CARPET TIPS FOR REAL-LIFE EVENTS

1. **CHOOSE SOMETHING TIMELESS** rather than trendy. Your money is much better spent investing in a great-quality dress that you can wear again and again, rather than on something that will look instantly dated.

2. **VINTAGE CAN BE A GREAT OPTION** if you're on a budget. People dressed up a lot more back in the day, so you can often get a dress with a ton of character without spending a fortune. Plus, you can trust that no one else will be wearing the same dress!

3. Very few things fit perfectly right off the rack. **ENLISTING THE HELP OF A TAILOR** for a couturelike fit isn't cheap, but it can elevate a dress from good enough to great.

4. You can have a perfect body and still benefit from a **BODY SHAPER**: They smooth out lines, hold your tummy in (even after a big meal), and are an extra layer of fabric between your skin and the camera's flash.

5. **GIVE YOURSELF A ONCE-OVER** before you leave the house and check for deodorant marks. You can usually remove these by rubbing the fabric against itself or using the foam part from the top of a drycleaning hanger to lift the stain. Better yet, use clear deodorant.

6. **DON'T FORGET ABOUT YOUR BODY** when you apply makeup. You never want a line of demarcation between the color of your face and the color of the rest of you, but you should take the time to apply either lotion and a bit of bronzer, or a shimmery self-tanner.

7. If you're working with a **FABRIC THAT'S A BIT SHEER**, make sure to take some photos of yourself *with* a flash to ensure that you're not accidentally showing anything that you don't want to show.

8. **MOVE AROUND IN YOUR DRESS** before you head out the door—make sure that you're not going to split it up the back the second you take your seat, and be sure you're not accidentally showing your body shaper or slip when you move around.

9. **CUT OUT THE RIBBON LOOPS** for hangers so they don't make an appearance under your arm. They can make a perfect dress look messy.

10. **PACK A LITTLE KIT IN YOUR PURSE** in case of on-the-road emergencies. Safety pins, a sewing kit, and double-stick tape are very helpful should you find yourself in a bathroom stall mending your dress.

* Give yourself
a once-over.

* Go for dramatic hair and a bold lip (see page 162 for the how-to).

ESTEE'S TIPS FOR PLAYING UP YOUR BODY SHAPE

Most of us aren't shaped like fit models, so it's important to throw the spotlight on the part of your body that you love the most. If it's your waist, go for a fuller skirt and a dress that's fitted through the middle to create an hourglass effect (a belt can amplify that). If you love your legs, find a fancy dress that's cocktail length; if your arms are lovely, go sleeveless.

The other factor that can hugely improve how well a dress fits is a great high-quality fabric. Also, well-tailored pieces are always more flattering and can do a lot to disguise any part of your body that you don't absolutely love. And speaking of the tailor, almost everything needs to be fitted to look its best. You can get a sense of how an alteration will change the shape by moving the hemline up and down to find the most flattering length (some women love their knees, while others don't). You can also raise or drop the waist until you find the ideal spot.

ESTEE'S TIPS FOR MAKING SOMETHING SIMPLE SPECIAL

1. The dress is just one part of the equation. Don't be afraid to pick something simple and GO FOR DRAMATIC HAIR AND A BOLD LIP.

2. You can get great wear out of a basic dress by SWAPPING IN ACCESSORIES. A big belt, bright shoes, or statement earrings can give it new life, again and again.

3. When you're accessorizing, DON'T GET TOO MATCHY. The belt doesn't need to match the shoes or the necklace. And pick one statement and let the other elements be barely there (or not there at all). If you go for a bejeweled belt, for example, choose a pair of nude or black heels; if you go for big earrings, don't feel compelled to wear a big necklace as well.

4. DRESS SOMETHING SIMPLE UP by adding a beaded cardigan or tuxedo jacket; DRESS SOMETHING DOWN by pairing it with a bomber jacket or leather blazer.

HOLLYWOOD GLAM

"Hello, gorgeous!"
—FANNY BRICE, *FUNNY GIRL*

Getting your face and hair prepped for a big event is pure fantasy: There's nothing quite like the power of hair and makeup to completely transform your look, to turn you into a character—a beach girl, a sophisticate, a Hollywood movie star. Hair and makeup artists can wipe away sleep deprivation, cowlicks, blemishes, damaged tresses, tired eyes, and even asymmetrical features—though if they focus on making you look "perfect," they've likely gone too far. Feeling confident about your hair, your makeup, and your dress is key when you step out for any big event, whether it's the prom, your

wedding, or opening night of a movie—but it's just as essential that you still look like you, rather than a totally different person. My hairstylist, Mark Townsend, and my makeup artist, Melanie Inglessis, always play up—rather than diminish—my most unique features.

When we're sitting in our hairstylist's chair at the salon or visiting with a makeup artist at a beauty counter at the mall, we're really at our most vulnerable: Here is someone who is assessing your face and hair from every angle, looking you up and down. Make sure that you pick people who celebrate all the wonderful things about your signature look rather than nitpick everything that should be fixed—and you also want to feel like they aren't attempting to change you. If you have curly hair, you don't need a haircut intended for someone who has stick-straight locks, for example. You want to leave your hairstylist's chair feeling your best, like they've assessed your hair and your lifestyle and given you a cut and style that really work for you. And while we don't all visit with makeup artists routinely, you should still find a pro at a beauty counter at your local department store whom you can turn to for help. You don't need someone who is looking to sell you a million things you don't need—you need someone who can teach you how to play up your eyes or lips with a few key products and tools. The drugstore is wonderful for everything else.

When you're looking for your pros, the key is to ask friends who have great style for their recommendations—and then, instead of booking a cut, go and see this potential stylist for something like a blowout first. That way you can get a sense of whether it feels like a good match, and you can feel out what they would do to your hair: If their suggestion feels like too much work (e.g., if you have five minutes to get ready in the morning and they want to give you a cut that requires a blow-dryer and curling iron) or they want to take your look in a direction that you don't feel comfortable with (long to short, etc.), then you should keep looking.

I found my people in much the same way: I met Melanie at my first *Glee* event, and we never stopped working together. I immediately fell in love with her because she put down her brushes and ran out to get me Spanx because I was in

a bind—and she's been taking care of me ever since. I feel so comfortable with her, she's really like a second mother. Not only does she make me look beautiful for all of my big moments, but spending time with her puts me in the right mood to step out on the red carpet. I trust that Melanie knows my face and will always make me look amazing, playing up my ethnicity in the process. Sometimes she'll even refuse to give me what I claim I want (More lip! More lash!) because she knows it won't play right. I've never left her chair looking like anyone other than a great version of myself. Part of that is letting me be in my twenties, too, by keeping my makeup pretty minimal: If you wear too much, you can age yourself pretty fast.

I met Mark shortly after I met Melanie. He's known for being one of the best stylists in town and does big, gorgeous Hollywood hair for some of the industry's most beautiful girls. He wanted to work with me and so he called my publicist, who told him, "That's fine, but you have to understand that Lea's very loyal and wants a team that's essentially a family," and he said, "You got it." He's never left my side. I feel so fortunate that he's stuck with me, despite all the pulls on his time. You should feel like your people care enough that they'll always make time for you— that if you need a quick bang trim, they'll never mind if you just pop into the salon.

Mark, Melanie, and I have the best time together: We laugh, we play music, we pass around inspiration shots. It's all so much fun that when

something theoretically stressful happens—like someone gets sick and we only have fifteen minutes to get ready, or we don't like the look and need to scratch it all and start over with only minutes to spare—it just makes it even better. We know one another so well that we can always roll with the punches. I'm so lucky to have them in my life.

In this chapter, Mark and Melanie break down the steps to achieve five of our favorite looks—we picked these in particular because they're easy enough to master at home, but they're still fun, fresh, and totally modern. And, as you'll see, there's a look for every occasion, from brunch with your friends to the most important of nights out on the town.

↑ *Mark, Melanie, and me at a photo shoot getting our glam on.*

GETTING YOUR MAKE-UP TO LAST ALL NIGHT

It's a big luxury to be able to travel with a hair-and-makeup team for red carpet events—when Mark and Melanie have to send me out on my own, they do what they can to ensure that my hair stays put (or looks even better as it becomes slightly undone) and that my makeup doesn't migrate down my face. Here are Melanie's tips for making makeup stick.

1. "If you have oily skin, avoid cream-based cosmetics. Instead, use a primer for the face, and also for the eyes, and then pick products that are matte and powder based. Ultimately, you need to create a canvas that makeup can stick to. There are also mattifying gels on the market, which you apply pre-makeup. They sink into the pores and are colorless, so you can avoid building up too much product."

2. "If you have dry skin, using too much powder can create a cakelike effect. Choose a liquid foundation and cream-based products, which you can then set with a tiny bit of pressed powder."

3. "If you'd like to do a really strong lip, apply a light concealer over the lips, and then powder it ever so slightly to set it. Then go over your mouth with a pencil, filling in the entire shape. Apply lipstick next, and gloss if you want a shim-mery finish. When you apply gloss, keep it in the center of your lips so it doesn't bleed out."

4. "It's key to ensure that the T-zone never gets shiny. You want your entire face to be dewy and fresh except for the T-zone. You can bring powder and pat it on (though it can get cakey if you apply too many layers), or you can pack blotting papers. Essentially, these are rice papers that absorb oil. So blot, then apply powder."

MAKEUP FOR PHOTOS

Whether you're facing down a row of cameras on the red carpet or your friend's iPhone at dinner, a flash can really wash out your face. If getting great pictures of an event is important (e.g., at a prom or a wedding), then you probably need more makeup than you think you do—if at all possible, speak with the photographer about their lighting, as different artists like different things . . . and their choices will transform your makeup dramatically. Regardless of the photo style, make sure that your T-zone isn't oily, that your hair isn't greasy, and that all blemishes are nicely covered. Low light, lamplight, and candlelight are all very flattering, while sunlight will make everything visible (including too much makeup). If you're prepping your face for day, make sure that your foundation is incredibly well blended (and as minimal as possible).

MELANIE'S BEAUTY SECRETS

1. **"Don't sleep with your makeup on.** It can be a drag to do your whole skin-cleansing ritual right before bed, so if that doesn't work for you, look into wipes, or wash your face after you get home from work or school while you still have the energy."

2. **"Exfoliate a few times a week.** If your skin is very sensitive, you can always mix your exfoliator with a gentle cleanser to make it less intense (or choose an exfoliator for sensitive skin). Clarisonics are great for daily use, too."

3. **"Drink plenty of water.** Good skin starts from the inside."

4. "To make sure that you always look dewy, **use an illuminating liquid foundation,** which I like to apply with a wet beauty blender. Don't use powder—if your skin is oily, then use a cream mattifying gel in lieu of powder."

5. **"Keep your eyebrows maintained:** They are like a hanger for your face, as all your features fall below them. They can really change your look and give you a very subtle face-lift. Don't overpluck, just keep them defined and groomed."

6. "I give 99 percent of my clients **a little dab of peach blush**—either cream or powder—right at the top of their cheekbones before they head out the door. Smile, and tap it on very gently. It adds an instant glow and air of health."

7. "If you have thin lips and want them to look a little fuller, pout, and **apply a lighter color right in the middle of your bow.**"

8. "If you want to play with false eyelashes, figure out which effect you're going for first—and **use single lashes for a more natural look.** If you have small eyes and want to open them, put the longest lashes in the middle; if you want to elongate your eyes, place the longest lashes at the ends."

9. **"Swap out your black mascara for brown mascara** when it's time to do your lower lashes. It will help to open up your eyes."

10. "To brighten the eyes, **use a peachy, off-white pencil** in the water line at the bottom only—it works on all skin tones."

11. **"Highlighter can really brighten the eye area.** Place a dab in the inner corner of the eye and a little right under the point of the eyebrow. It can be a cream or a powder."

Before I step out onto a red carpet or make my way to a big event, Mark and Melanie always take my picture—using a flash—so we can see how the look is translating. I urge you to do the same thing if you want to commemorate an event in photos. That way, you can tweak your look and have no regrets.

PREPPING YOUR FACE

It can be tempting to rush straight to the fun stuff, but prepping your face properly for makeup is more important than everything else that comes after. You need a gorgeous blank canvas with which to work, and you want your skin to look as beautiful and glowing as possible. Here's how Melanie gets faces ready for prime time.

1. **MOISTURIZER.** "Take the time to find the right moisturizer for your skin type—it should be rich enough to work but never goopy, greasy, or too thick."

2. **PRIMER.** "If you have problematic skin or oily skin, you might want to use a primer before you apply foundation: This will smooth out your skin and allow the foundation to glide on easier."

3. **FOUNDATION.** "Apply foundation from the center of your face outward, so that by the time you reach your neck, there's very little product left and it will blend perfectly. You can use a brush, a sponge, or your fingers—go with what makes you feel most comfortable and helps you achieve a flawless, streak-free finish."

4. **CONCEALER.** "For blemishes, take a tiny brush and pat concealer directly on the area needed. The concealer should be a perfect match to your skin tone. For the under-eye area, use either a flat brush or your ring finger (the warmth of your finger helps to blend the concealer). Immediately below (right above the cheekbone), I tap on highlighter and apply in a similar way. Using my ring finger, I pat and roll, moving to the outer corner and lifting up."

5. **EYEBROW BRUSH.** "The perfect eyebrow shape is key, so keep them strong and groomed (don't overpluck!). Using an eyebrow brush, gently stroke them up and over."

6. **CONTOURING.** "Using a liquid foundation that's a few shades darker than your normal foundation color, you'll want to blend under your cheekbones, under the jawline, and at the top of the forehead. Work slowly and with small quantities of foundation. You can always add more to build up the color—you want to add definition that looks very natural. If you're using a powder foundation, use a powder foundation to contour; the same holds if it's liquid or cream. Keeping the finish consistent is key."

Melanie's Tips for Finding the Right Foundation

1. "Department store lights have little in common with natural light. After you apply the shade, walk outside to see how it looks in normal life."

2. "Don't test shades on your hand, which can often be significantly darker than your face. Instead, test shades on your jawline—the right color will blend into your neck perfectly."

3. "Most people's skin tone is somewhere in between two shades of foundation, particularly as the year evolves. Buy two shades and mix them together, changing your formulation as you get more or less sun through the seasons."

4. "If you have clear skin and don't need a lot of coverage, buy a tinted moisturizer; alternately, you can mix your foundation with a bit of moisturizer or illuminizer to dilute its opacity."

MARK TOWNSEND'S BEAUTY SECRETS

1. "I ask all my clients to wash their hair only every three days. When you wash your hair every day, you're stripping the strands of their natural oils, so your scalp overproduces oil to compensate. You can still take a shower and get your head wet, just don't use shampoo: Instead massage your scalp with your hands so the water moves the oil down the strands. If you have bangs, go ahead and separate them from the rest of your hair and wash daily. Eventually, your scalp will produce less oil so you won't feel so greasy."

2. "Everyone should own some dry shampoo, which either has powder or starch in it. This absorbs oil, so you can spray dry shampoo on your roots, massage it in, and then brush it through. It's also amazing for adding texture and building volume that lasts. If you just need a touch-up after a long day of work or school, flip your head over, spray, and then scrunch it up. Dry shampoo gives your style that coveted second-day texture but will still keep your hair looking clean."

3. "I ask all of my clients to do my restorative hair masque (see page 56 for recipe) weekly, ideally for an hour at a time (they throw it on while they take a bath or put a shower cap over their head and do other things around the house). The reason I use coconut oil is that its molecules are tiny and can penetrate the hair shaft; most other oils can't get into the hair shaft and just sit on top. They're sealing the cuticle, which is great, but they're not giving you the benefits of tons of moisture."

4. "There's nothing sadder than hair that can't move: It should be soft and very touchable. So instead of spraying your entire head with hair spray, spot-treat flyaways by spritzing a natural-bristle toothbrush (it cannot be plastic) with a flexible-hold hair spray and touching up out-of-control strands."

5. "I cut my clients' hair every twelve weeks—no more, unless they have a short haircut or a bob that has a very specific shape that needs maintenance (in which case, every six weeks). By stretching it out between cuts, you can preserve your length. Invest in a really great quarterly cut rather than more frequent trims—it's definitely worth the money to style from a good base."

6. "A lot of the blow-dryers on the market get too hot, so when you're blowing out your hair, be careful to protect it. Rough-dry your hair until it's 90 percent dry (i.e., don't focus the nozzle directly on the strands) before you start pulling on it with a brush—and never, ever flat-iron wet or damp hair."

BLOWING OUT YOUR HAIR

Mark prefers it when I go a few days before washing my hair so that it has plenty of texture for him to work with, but I hate skipping a shampoo, so he'll use some dry shampoo to add texture (see previous page). Here's how he gets my hair prepped for more intensive styling.

1. "I always blow out bangs while they're wet before I do anything else—and I never apply product to them. Because bangs are touched constantly, they can get greasy fast. Hold the blow-dryer from above so that the air is pushing them down, as you don't want any volume in the front."

2. "I divide hair into two sections, top and bottom, and then pin the top half up."

3. "Taking a dime-size amount of anti-frizz product, I rub it in my hands and then apply it to damp hair, working it evenly and thoroughly through the strands. It's key that you divide the hair into sections (top and bottom each get a dime-size amount) so that you don't overdistribute product to the top section, weighing it down. Ultimately, frizz starts underneath, on areas of the hair that are often neglected."

4. "Start by blowing out the top section first. This is by far the most exhausting for your arms, and they'll get tired fast, so save your strength to use here as this hair is also the most visible. Use a round brush as you blow to smooth it out, and then clip it back up. You can rough-dry the bottom section since it's not as important—once it's nearly dry, take a round brush and smooth it out as you finish it off."

MY FIVE FAVORITE MAJOR BEAUTY LOOKS

DATE NIGHT
SMOKY EYE + NUDE LIP

1. Rim the entire eye with a soft kohl pencil. Kohl is a little messy, so it doesn't have to be perfect (you can tidy it up after with a Q-tip that's been dipped in makeup remover). Use your finger or a pointed brush to smudge the line—you can also find a kohl pencil that has a sponge on the end.

2. Finish the eye by taking a cream eye shadow in the shade you prefer (taupe, bronze, gray) and working it into the crease with a pointy crease brush. Don't get too high or too far out with the color. Next, curl your lashes. And then take your mascara wand and wiggle it a bit at the base of the lashes as you move up. This ensures that you separate and coat the lashes for optimal coverage. On the bottom lashes, hold the mascara wand vertically and apply like a windshield wiper.

3. Using a cream blush, smile, and pat the color on the apple of the cheek to add freshness. You'll want to tap and then blend, adding color gradually until it looks just right.

4. Because the eyes are dramatic, you'll want to keep your lips nude. Take a matte cream lip stain or lipstick and using your finger, pat it on.

DATE NIGHT
BEACHY WAVE

1. Taking sections of hair that are four inches wide, roll hair under with a one-and-three-quarter-inch curling iron, and then set with a clip. Make sure to leave the bottom two inches of hair uncurled to make the wave a bit cooler and messier. If you're not great with a curling iron or need a shortcut, you can use one-and-three-quarter-inch hot rollers instead. Leave the curls clipped until they're no longer hot (hair "sets" as it cools).

2. Spray a paddle brush with flexible- or working-hold hair spray, remove the clips, and brush hair out.

3. Modern shapes are all about volume at the crown and ends of the hair, not at the front, so leave the front sections of hair alone. Take a teasing comb, lift a one-inch section of hair straight up, and then back-comb from halfway up the shaft all the way down to the root, about four times. Once you've applied enough volume, smooth it out with the comb.

4. Warm a light styling cream up in your hands and then run it through the hair, working the curls to create pieces and a sexy, tousled effect.

RED CARPET
GOLDEN GLOBES MAKEUP

1. Use a kohl liner along the top only—make the line as clean as possible and then wing it a tiny bit. Apply a small amount of shimmery dark brown eye shadow to a domed brush and then feather the line back and forth a bit. Apply two coats of mascara to the top, wiggling the wand at the base of the lashes as you move up. Use a dark brown mascara on the bottom lashes (apply vertically, like a windshield wiper) to open the eyes up a bit and to keep the overall effect nice and romantic.

2. Using either a cream or powder highlight that's shimmery pink or shimmery gold, highlight under the top of the eyebrow (right where it peaks) and also at the inner corner of the eye.

3. Taking a blush brush, apply a soft pink blush on the apple of the cheek, patting and swiping as you move up the cheekbone. Work gradually and lightly. It's much easier to add more blush than to have to take it off and start over.

4. Use a lip pencil to define the lips in a nice, soft pink, feathering it inside the lip a little bit so it's not a hard line. Add a super-high-shine gloss in pink to finish the look.

RED CARPET
GOLDEN GLOBES HAIR

1. Part hair to the side, and then, using a three-quarter-inch curling iron, curl everything forward toward the face, creating uneven waves as you go.

2. Make a horseshoe section of hair up top—essentially everything from the front to the crown of the head—and clip it for later. Then gather all the hair from the sides and pull to the center of the back of the head. Braid this hair, which is key for taming lots of layers and adding texture, and then secure with a little elastic at the end. Twist the braid into a bun, and put your first bobby pins through the elastic, forming an X. Moving around the bun, affix it to your head with X's of bobby pins. This anchors the look and will keep your hair from slipping.

3. Rub a light-hold styling cream in your hands and run it through the top section of hair to create pieceyness, then push hair forward over the bangs or forehead before bringing it back. If any loose tendrils are longer than chin length, pin them back into the chignon.

4. Take a reusable mascara wand and spray it with a flexible-hold hair spray. Work around your hairline and neck, cleaning the look up as you go. The mascara wand is key for very small amounts of hair that need to be tucked into a chignon. Flyaways are fine up top, but you don't want any around your ears.

SUNDAY BRUNCH
GLOWY BRONZER + COLORFUL EYES

1. Take a big bronzer brush and sweep across your cheeks, forehead, nose, and ultimately neck. Build gradually, shaking off as much product as possible before applying. It's much easier to add more than to start over!

2. Using a cream color base and a flat eye shadow brush, gently pat a wash of fun color across your lid, building up the density of the color gradually. Violet, blue, green, and pink are all fair game. Then take a shimmery powder of the same color and pat more on. The shimmery powder will stick to the cream base beneath.

3. Take a mascara in the same color family and wiggle the wand back and forth underneath the top lashes, to work the color throughout. Apply mascara to the bottom lashes by holding the wand vertically and swiping it like a windshield wiper.

4. Apply a light pink gloss to the lips, skipping liner.

SUNDAY BRUNCH
MESSY BRAID WITH NATURAL TEXTURE

1. Take a bit of light styling cream or lotion in your hands, warm it up, and then rake it through your hair to give a little hold and glossiness.

2. Pull all your hair behind one of your ears (whichever you prefer), and then create a classic three-strand braid. Secure with an elastic.

3. Tie a bit of ribbon at the bottom in a knot, not a bow—a slightly undone knot is best because a bow will look too precious on a braid that isn't supposed to look perfect.

4. You don't want a lot of loose hair around the front of your face, so spritz hair spray onto a natural-bristle toothbrush and clean up any flyaways. The toothbrush is better than a reusable mascara wand when you are looking to tidy hair (rather than tuck it into an updo).

BUSINESS MEETING
WINGED LINER + BERRY LIP

1. Before you apply liquid liner, angle your face up while looking in the mirror, and then stretch your eyelid to the side so it's smooth and taut. Start about halfway across your lash line, pushing the liquid liner as close as possible. Apply light pressure to draw your line, increasing thickness as you move to the outer corner of the eye. Once you've reached the outside corner of the eye, look straight into the mirror and wing up the liner with a flick. Then carefully connect the wing to the rest of the liner. The more aggressive the wing, the more retro the look.

2. Take a pointy Q-tip and douse it in a little eye makeup remover. While looking at yourself in the mirror, refine and sharpen the wing. Clean up any mess. If you want, you can take a little brush and face powder and tidy it even more. Then apply a lot of mascara, wiggling from the base of the lashes up.

3. Take a blush brush and a very neutral, understated blush that is matte and has no shimmer or glitter, and brush it across your cheeks. Don't make it too specific or too concentrated; instead you want something that's slightly more amped than your normal skin tone.

4. Pout your lips, and apply a berry-colored lip stain with your ring finger. Don't use a lip pencil, and don't finish the look with a gloss.

BUSINESS MEETING
SIDE PART, STRAIGHT

1. Divide hair into a top and bottom section. Secure the top, and take a dime-size amount of anti-frizz serum in your hands, rub together, and then evenly distribute. Repeat with top section. Don't apply any other products if you want your hair to last as long as possible.

2. Blow-dry hair roughly; when hair is 90 percent dry use a round brush while blow-drying to smooth it out.

3. Take two-inch sections of hair and slowly move a comb through the strands immediately in front of a flat iron. While the tendency is to try to straight-iron bigger sections to save time, this will actually cause damage. When you work with sections that are too large, you have to move the iron through your hair many times, frying the hairs on the outer edge in the process (and failing to get to the hairs in the middle). Instead, you'll want to move the iron through each two-inch section twice, max. While using smaller sections may seem like it would take longer, it's just as fast since you don't have to cover the same ground repeatedly.

4. Take a natural-bristle toothbrush, spritz it with hair spray, and smooth any flyaways.

DINNER WITH THE GIRLS
FUN LIP + SIMPLE EYE

1. Fill the entire lip with a bright pink lip pencil.

2. Apply an intensely pigmented lip lacquer. A bright lip needs to be super-precise so that it doesn't look sloppy, so dip a Q-tip in makeup remover and tidy up the edges. Finally, take a little brush and some face powder and carefully set the edge of the lip.

3. Take a powder brush and apply a powder illuminizer all over your face to give it a glow—pick a light pink or peach shade with a little shimmer.

4. Apply two coats of mascara, wiggling the wand from the base of the lashes up.

DINNER WITH THE GIRLS
HIGH BUN

1. Gather your hair at the crown of your head (not the top), and secure it in a ponytail with a very tight elastic. Spritz a paddle brush with working- or flexible-hold hair spray and smooth the hair up to the elastic, ensuring that it lies nice and flat.

2. Braid the ponytail and secure it with a second elastic.

3. Take your thumb and place it on the top of your head in front of the ponytail. Wrap the braid over the top of your thumb (toward your face), and then wrap under and tuck the end in.

4. Take bobby pins and place them through the elastic in an X formation, securing the bun to your head. Place X-formation bobby pins throughout the bun to anchor it in place.

The Spotlight

1. Don't try to make yourself look like everyone else—and don't use hair and makeup to disguise your uniqueness. Instead, play up what makes you you!

2. Find a hairstylist and someone who can help you with your makeup whom you really trust—you need someone who is excited to play up your distinctiveness. While it's great to bring in some professional help for big events, it's worth it to find someone—your mom, a good friend—who can help you learn how to do your makeup for every day.

3. Mark, Melanie, and I always confer about what gets to be the star of the show before I sit down in the hair-and-makeup chair. Are you going to do a really fun hairstyle, like a cool braid? Then maybe your makeup should take the backseat. Having too many things going on at once can be overwhelming—unless of course you're heading out to a big event.

4. If you tend to style your hair a lot, make sure that you're not damaging it with too much heat—don't pull on it with brushes, and don't rush to straighten it when it might still be damp. Every weekend, take the time to nourish it with a hair masque.

5. You won't enjoy your big night out if you're constantly having to redo or worry about your hair and makeup: Choose a hairstyle that's touchable (i.e., not too much hair spray) and will look better and better as it becomes more undone as the night progresses; make sure that you apply your makeup in such a way that it will last all night.

← Clockwise from top left: With my beautiful girlfriends Jamie, Joanna, and Stephanie ✳ me and the girls at my twenty-fifth birthday ✳ with Skyler Astin and Lauren Pritchard, some of my _Spring Awakening_ buddies ✳ a selfie with Stephanie on a quick trip to New York ✳ with my bestie, Chris Colfer, at my twenty-fifth birthday ✳ at the Hollywood Haunted Ride with Jennifer and Stephanie—an action shot before we quickly headed for the exit! ✳ with the girls in Santa Barbara on a girls' weekend getaway.

FRIENDSHIP

"What is exciting is not for one person to be stronger than the other but for two people to have met their match and yet they are equally as stubborn, as obstinate, as passionate, as crazy as the other."
— BARBRA STREISAND

As I've mentioned, creating and maintaining close friendships has always been difficult for me: Throughout my life, I've been too occupied with work. But when I moved to Los Angeles, far from my family, I knew that I would need a support system on the West Coast. I am so grateful that I've developed some incredibly strong relationships, because if I've learned anything from the very difficult experience of losing someone, having wonderful friends around you is the most important thing there is. While it's your family's duty to be there for you, seeing how my friends showed up when Cory passed was simply amazing: They put their own lives on hold to put me first. They were with me every night; they stopped by every morning; they checked in with me all day, every day, to make sure that I was hanging in there. You hope that you will never need to lean on your friends in that way, but it is a powerful feeling to know that you can and that they'll be there for you in your darkest times of need.

It's hard to believe that five years ago, this circle did not exist. When I arrived in Los Angeles, I didn't know a soul on the West Coast, which was both terrifying and lonely. Fortunately, in my first week there, I met Stephanie, a woman who ultimately became one of my best friends and introduced me to a small network of incredible people. And I just so happened to meet her on one of the scariest days of my life. I was in Los Angeles for my final *Glee* audition when I got into a terrible car accident on Pico, right outside of the Fox lot. The crash was like an out-of-body experience: The only thing I remember is leaving my totaled car in the middle of the street (the Fox security team told me they'd take care of it) and running up the lot and straight into my audition, where word of what just happened had already reached the casting director. They told me to go home and that I could audition another day, but I said absolutely not, that I was there to audition for Rachel Berry, and audition I would. I asked for two minutes in the ladies' room to pull myself together and ducked out the door.

I went to the bathroom, where I appraised my appearance in the mirror. I looked like a mess. And then in walked a quintessential blond California girl of my age, who was a Fox intern who worked in casting. She recognized me from the audition room and asked if I needed anything. I told her that if she helped me get ready, I'd take her out to lunch the next day. She picked glass out of my hair, she wiped the blood from the cuts on my face, and most important of all, she gave me some lip gloss. That day, I got the job of my life and a new best friend. I recognize that it doesn't always happen that way and that I'm incredibly lucky to have walked right into my circle of friends. It can take a long time to meet great people, but it's essential to persevere—and remember that quality is always better than quantity.

One of the reasons that Stephanie and I have remained so close—which is the same reason I'm close to all of my friends—is that we both prefer to live very quiet lives. All my friends are the same way. They're not L.A. party girls—they're all as driven and focused on their respective careers as I am. We have very different personalities—some of us are more outspoken, some are more sensitive—but the unifying force is that we're all strong and centered. All of my friends have great jobs and are much more interested in pouring energy into their personal lives than in partying it up on the club scene. On the nights when we all get to hang out together, you'll usually find us on the couch, ordering food and watching *The Bachelor*. My favorite thing about these nights is that they're so simple: We really don't need much—outside of each other—to have fun. As uneventful as that may seem, those truly might be the best nights ever.

FUN NIGHTS WITH GIRLFRIENDS

While girls' night in always ranks high, we're not always camped out in one of our houses, rotating DJ responsibilities and ordering in. Here are some of the other things we like to do together:

1. **TRYING NEW RESTAURANTS.** Have I mentioned that I love food? I wish we could do as the girls on *Sex and the City* do and find our version of the diner, but alas, it doesn't happen every week. We do make a huge effort to see each other as much as possible, though.

2. **GOING TO THE SPA.** Massages are much more fun when you can make a girls' event out of them.

3. **GOING TO CONCERTS.** Every few months we'll all get online and see what concerts are coming to town. We make it a point to get tickets well in advance and write it in our calendars in pen. Rihanna on tour? Check.

4. **ROAD TRIPS.** A vacation doesn't have to mean getting on a plane and heading to a tropical destination. We've had some of our greatest times together right outside of Los Angeles. Often, after a particularly long or stressful week, we'll make a game-time decision, hop into the car, and head to Ojai or Santa Barbara for some group self-care time. We'll sit by the hotel pool, take some yoga classes, and generally have fun taking care of ourselves, together.

IT'S SO IMPORTANT, & SO COMFORTING, TO HAVE LAMPPOSTS IN THIS WORLD WHO CAN LIGHT THE WAY.

Clockwise from top left: With Stephanie at <u>X Factor</u> in 2012 ✳ with Jennifer in Mexico ✳ Stephanie and me in 2012.

SIX FRIENDSHIP NO-NOS

1. If you feel like you can't be yourself, something is wrong with the friendship. Not only should you feel like yourself when you're together, but your friends should make you feel like the best version of yourself.

2. There should be reciprocation. Just as you'd do anything for the people you love, you should expect the same from them. My friends would get up in the middle of the night to be there for me; I would make the same sacrifice for the people I love.

3. Your friends should want the best for you. A lot of my friends are actresses, and that could be considered an uncomfortable or a competitive thing. Sometimes we might even be up for some of the same roles, which you'd think would be awkward. It's not: We truly want each other to get the role as much as we want it for ourselves. Might seem impossible to believe, but it's true.

4. If someone's malicious, they're not the right friend for you. Love and support are the basis of any long-lasting friendship—it can be impossible to recover from harsh and unkind words. This doesn't mean that you can't express the things that bother you about each other, but if it's done in a way that feels undeniably mean, that's not okay.

5. Betrayal is never okay. My friends and I have a code word that we say to each other that means that nothing we say can leave the room. If you have a friend who is betraying that circle of trust, then they're not a good friend. You need to know that you can feel safe to say and do whatever you need to do around those you're closest with.

6. Not letting things go. Even though I'm an outspoken person and never shy about expressing how I feel, I get very nervous when I get into arguments with friends. I hate feeling like there's anything coming between me and a good friend, and so I always make the effort to call, reach out, or go over to give them a big hug. It can be scary, but it's always worth putting an argument behind us so that it doesn't become a bigger deal than it actually is.

LOVE LETTER TO JONATHAN GROFF

When I decided to write this book, I knew I couldn't do it without devoting an entire section to Jonathan Groff. He's my best friend in the entire world—in fact, it's fair to say that I didn't understand the concept until I met him. He's been through more ups and downs with me than anyone else. He's like a brother, and I love him like crazy.

We met at our *Spring Awakening* audition. I had done workshops of the show, so I felt pretty confident that I'd be able to keep my role with the production, but we needed to find a guy to play Melchior. And in walked Jonathan Groff, this kid from Lancaster, Pennsylvania, wearing jeans that were way too short and a shirt that had clearly been washed when it needed to have been dry-cleaned. And the gel! His hair was as hard as a rock. I looked at him and thought, "What a sweet boy, but he's never going to get this part." But I helped him that day because it was clear that he was the nicest person: I gave him some insight into things the director liked to see and worked through some of the scenes with him outside the room before we went in. But I can't take much credit because there was a huge amount of talent beneath the badly fitting outfit and hair gel! Not only did he get the part, but he ended up getting a Tony nomination and the launchpad for an incredibly successful career.

To this day, I've never met someone who has understood me more than Jonathan—I can completely be myself, with all my different quirks, and never feel judged. I've laughed harder, and cried harder, with Jonathan

I'm eternally grateful to Jonathan for always helping me keep my feet on the ground.

than I have with anyone else. We've been kicked out of Broadway shows for falling into fits of giggles in the audience, and I've literally shown up on his doorstep with my heart broken. He

always helps me put myself together. After one particularly rough episode with a guy, Jonathan wrote me this incredibly nice letter, in which he told me that I would find someone amazing. He was going away on a vacation and so he gave me a task to complete while he was gone, since he knew I would miss him like crazy and needed distractions. He instructed me to watch every single Meryl Streep movie while he was gone—and said that there would be a quiz when he returned.

And then there was the time we went to Washington, DC, together so that I could sing for President Obama. Melanie was there in the hotel room with us, doing my makeup, and I was trying to focus on the task at hand; serenading the leader of the free world is no small thing. But Jonathan was intent on getting me to laugh, and so a wrestling match/tickle fest went too far, and he made me laugh so hard I peed my pants. I assure you, I showered—but thirty short minutes later, I was in front of the president. Those are the moments that keep you sane, and so I'm eternally grateful to Jonathan for always helping me

keep my feet on the ground. If peeing my pants is what it takes, I'm always game.

From the moment I met Jonathan, I knew that he was gay. I've always been a loud and outspoken person who has little to no filter. But for whatever reason, even though I would normally not have been shy about saying, "Oh, you're gay," out loud in front of other people (particularly Broadway people), with Jonathan, I held my tongue. I didn't want to do or say anything that might possibly hurt or embarrass him, particularly because it was apparent that he wasn't ready to be out. For the first time, I could feel someone's emotions. I could feel that at that time, he just wasn't ready, and I needed to give him the space to do it on his own.

We call ourselves City Mouse and Country Mouse, because he grew up with Amish people, while I grew up with cross-dressers in New York City. Watching Jonathan grow over the years has been one of the best things ever: He's developed an incredible career and been a wonderful son to his parents (now my parents' best friends).

← Jonathan and me at the Spring Awakening Tony Awards—we had such an amazing time that night, and this is now one of my favorite pictures.

That time in *Spring Awakening* with Jonathan was the best time of my life. We had a very intense sex scene that we had to do together; you have to feel really comfortable with someone to do that. We went there together, every night. Sometimes we would do the scene and cry the entire time; others, we would be silly and laugh. But we were in it together.

I also have Jonathan to thank for *Glee*. Jonathan was in Los Angeles filming a TV pilot with Ryan Murphy when I went through a bad breakup (yes, same bad breakup that I've mentioned before—ha ha, if you're reading this, and thanks for getting me my big break!). I needed to get out of NYC and spend some time with Jon, so I flew to L.A. to see him. After I arrived, Jonathan, Ryan, and I went to Chateau Marmont, and I spent the night talking to Ryan about how much I love and admire Barbra Streisand. After, Jonathan told me that Ryan was writing a show called *Glee* and that he wanted me to do it. I was like, "Yeah, right—I'm never going to get that," as I hadn't had any luck breaking into TV.

I'm so thankful for him—obviously for introducing me to Ryan and pointing me toward *Glee*, but mainly because he's there for me like no one else and it's such a relief to know that a person like Jonathan is out there.

NIGHT-IN FAVORITES

I really love to cook, but in a fairly simple way. When friends come over, I don't always pull out all the stops—while my friends don't need me to impress them with culinary fireworks, I find that these easy-to-make recipes delight nonetheless. Down-home favorites are the best complement to a comfy night at home.

Egg in a Hole

Eating breakfast for dinner is the greatest break in routine and *always* feels fun. This is my Italian take on a croque-madame.

....

1. Drizzle the olive oil in a heavy skillet and set it over medium heat.

2. Take the piece of bread and scoop out an indent in the center with a spoon (it shouldn't go all the way through).

3. Sprinkle the bread with sea salt and grill it in the pan on both sides.

4. Crack an egg into the indent, cover the pan, and cook for about 2 minutes (you don't want the egg to be fully cooked before you flip it).

5. Using a spatula, flip the bread and egg together, and let it cook for 1 minute more.

6. Flip it again and put some roasted red peppers and a slice of your favorite cheese (I really like Manchego) on top, cover, and cook until the cheese melts, about 1 minute.

1 tablespoon olive oil

1 slice country bread, 1½ inches thick

Pinch of sea salt

1 egg

¼ cup jarred roasted red peppers, drained and sliced

1 slice Manchego or your favorite cheese

NOTE: If you don't want to make this in a pan, invest in a panini press. It's one of the best tools in my kitchen, because you can make gourmet, professional-looking sandwiches in less than five minutes. If you make your egg in a hole this way, you'll need a second piece of bread to top it.

Vegan Jalapeño Grilled Cheese Sandwich

This is sneakily healthy! You can use regular cheese, obviously, but I've found that most people don't know the difference!

....

1. Place a frying pan or heavy skillet over medium-high heat.

2. Spread the margarine on one side of each slice of bread.

3. On the opposite sides, add a thin layer of cream cheese.

4. Place one slice of bread, cream cheese side up, in the pan, and top with the pepper Jack cheese. Grill, open side up.

5. Once the cheese has melted, add the jalapeño.

6. Top with the second slice of bread, cream cheese side down, and flip the sandwich. Keep grilling, flipping until the sandwich is nice and brown.

2 slices Ezekiel bread

2 teaspoons vegan margarine (or regular margarine)

2 tablespoons vegan cream cheese (or regular cream cheese)

3 slices vegan pepper Jack cheese (or regular cheese)

1 or 2 teaspoons jalapeño, seeded and minced (see Note)

NOTE: If you like a lot of spice, you can cut the jalapeño into very thin rounds. Be careful not to burn your mouth. . . . Never touch your eyes immediately after handling a hot pepper, and always wash your hands immediately after touching one!

Mediterannean Nachos

One of the wonderful things about a concept like nachos is that it pretty much works with any sort of toppings that you want. I like this version with blue corn chips and hummus. You will need to modify the ingredients for the amount of nachos you want to make (it's easy to make enough to feed a big crowd).

....

1. Preheat the oven to 400°F.

2. Place the chips on a baking sheet.

3. Add dollops of hummus (this doesn't need to be precise or perfect).

4. Sprinkle onion, peppers, and black olives across the top (you can sauté these first, if you like, though I like them crunchy).

5. Cover the top with pepper Jack cheese.

6. Bake until the cheese melts, about 3 minutes.

7. Sprinkle the crumbled feta on top. Add a few dashes of Tapatío Hot Sauce, if you like things spicy.

Blue corn chips

Hummus

Onion, chopped

Red bell pepper, chopped

Yellow bell pepper, chopped

Black olives, chopped

Pepper Jack cheese, grated

Feta cheese, crumbled

Tapatío Hot Sauce (optional)

WHY COOKING FOR FRIENDS IS THE BEST

If you haven't noticed, cooking is very important to me—it's one of the biggest ways that I display love for people. My favorite thing to do is to open my home to friends and show them how much I care through home-cooked meals. While it's always nice to text and call and reach out to make sure that all of your friends are doing well, it's always important to make an extra effort—making everyone dinner is so much more special than hitting a local restaurant. It takes time and energy, but it's so worth it.

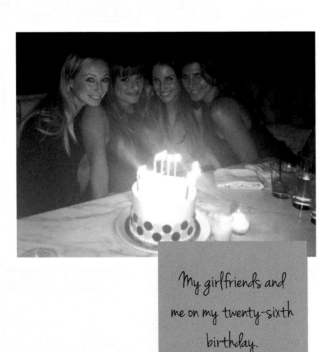

My girlfriends and me on my twenty-sixth birthday.

The Spotlight

1. In times of need, your relationships really get tested. Whether it's something as intense as loss or just needing someone to talk to in the middle of the night, it's those times when you see who is really there for you.

2. You don't need to have a night out on the town to have a fun night with friends. I find that I have way better relationships with friends who are happy to just relax at home.

3. Good friends are hard to find. Take your time developing those relationships. It's more important to have a few good friends than a thousand minor acquaintances. Work on your friendships in the same way you'd tackle anything of importance in your life. And be judicious about the special people you let into your circle.

4. You don't need to impress your friends. You should always feel like you can be yourself, without judgment.

5. Your best friend network is your family. Take care of your relationships with your relatives the same way that you care for your closest girlfriends.

Ten Movies to Watch with the Girls

Funny Girl
(Because it's about Fanny Brice's struggle between her passion for the stage and passion for a man she loves.)

500 Days of Summer

Katy Perry: Part of Me
(Although it's a movie about her music career, it really does show the arc of her relationship, which is something I found to be very relatable and personal. My friends and I *love* watching this movie together. I've watched it about seven times.)

Can't Hardly Wait

The Princess Bride
(Duh Obsessed.)

Clueless

Heathers

Marie Antoinette

Jawbreaker

Overboard

MY TOP TEN MOVIE SNACKS

1. Popcorn with truffle salt

2. Grapes

3. Chocolate-covered goji berries

4. Pop chips

5. Seaweed paper

6. Yogurt-covered strawberries

7. Vegan chocolate coconut ice cream

8. Gummy bears

9. Chocolate-covered blueberries

10. Teriyaki-spiced nuts

MY LIFE WITH GLEE

"To have ego means to believe in your own strength. And to also be open to other people's views. It is to be open, not closed. So, yes, my ego is big, but it's also very small in some areas. My ego is responsible for my doing what I do—bad or good."
—BARBRA STREISAND

I grew up on the Broadway stage, and because of this, Broadway always felt like home—I knew I could probably always find a place there. And while that really was good enough for me, I was always curious about TV and movies and continued to audition for other things. Despite my best efforts over the years, and even though I was climbing the proverbial ladder on Broadway, I never managed to book anything big. This wasn't upsetting so much as discouraging: Casting directors frequently told me that I wasn't pretty enough for TV, that I was too ethnic to ever be mainstream. One manager told me that as soon as I got my period and

was, accordingly, old enough for plastic surgery, I should get my nose done immediately. After hearing these sorts of suggestions from decision makers enough times, I started to believe them. And since I wasn't going to get plastic surgery or change the way I looked, I figured I'd stick to a life on the stage, where I had always been accepted. I did a little spot on *Third Watch*, and I did a few small parts on soap operas when I was younger, but other than that, it was the theater for me.

But just as those managers were wrong to tell me that I'd never make it outside of Broadway, I was just as wrong to believe them, since the fact that I don't look like everyone else is exactly what's opened the most doors for me. The industry has changed a lot since then—there's a lot more diversity in terms of who gets to be a leading lady—and I think that shows like *Glee* really put that trend in motion.

As I mentioned, when I was doing *Spring Awakening* with Jonathan Groff, he introduced me to Ryan Murphy—who later professed to be writing a script called *Glee* with me in mind. Even though it supposedly had my name on it, I figured they would ultimately give it to someone like Vanessa Hudgens, who was in the midst of *High School Musical* fame. I just had locked into my head the idea that I wasn't castable. A few Broadway stars had crossed over at that point, one of my favorites being Tony winner Sara Ramirez, who was on *Grey's Anatomy*. I thought that I wouldn't be a leading lady like her, but that maybe I could get some smaller roles. Maybe.

After *Spring Awakening* wrapped up, it seemed wise to step away for a little while. When you do something that big, that gets that much acclaim, you need to let the waters settle for a little bit. I was offered the role of Eponine in a *Les Misérables* production in Los Angeles at the Hollywood Bowl, and since I'd only ever been to L.A. once (to visit Jonathan, when I first met Ryan), I thought it might be a good opportunity for me to audition for some TV shows. After all, maybe once a year you find a Broadway show, like *The Book of Mormon,* that manages to get big outside of the theater community—and that year, *Spring Awakening* was it, so I thought I had enough credibility from the show to get some meetings with casting directors, and I wanted to capitalize on that. Really, all I wanted was to play a car crash victim on *Grey's Anatomy,* mainly because it was my favorite show on TV.

While I was doing *Les Mis* at the Hollywood Bowl, I got the call that they wanted to see me for *Glee*. I remember reading the script for the first time and in that last scene, when the kids start singing "Don't Stop Believin'," I could hear the song in my head as I read, and I got chills. I just knew. I knew the show was going to be *huge*.

Even though I myself was having trouble

believing that I would actually land the role, the minute I read the part of Rachel Berry, I knew nobody could play her better than me. It's as if she had lived inside of me for my entire life. We're not the same person, but I completely understood who she was and what she was all about. I could access everything about her.

When I went in for my first audition, I thought it went terribly: The piano player messed up, and so I asked him to stop midway through the song and go back. I had to do a scene where Rachel slaps Finn (it was cut from the pilot). The casting director played Finn opposite me and in the moment, I accidentally slapped him for real. Inside, I was freaking out that I was bombing in real time, but little did I know, I was Rachel Berry in those moments. Rachel Berry is the one who stopped the piano player and slapped the casting director. It was all so her. When you ask Ryan, or any of the others who were in the room that day, they will tell you that it was clear. In fact, I was the only girl they saw for the role, at both the production studio and at Fox, the network.

Before my second audition, which was for Fox, I got into the infamous car accident. That day, I sang "Not for the Life of Me" from *Thoroughly Modern Millie* and "On My Own" from *Les Misérables*. Ryan had told me that if he thought it wasn't looking good for me in there, he would intervene and tell them that I was his first choice. After I got the part, he confessed that not only had he not intervened, but the network execs didn't even know that he knew me. I got the role completely on my own. I was so proud to know that I earned it.

After my audition, the casting director sent me out to the waiting room. And then they called me back in to tell me that the role was mine, which is definitely unusual. They rarely call you back into the room to deliver the news in person. I was so happy I screamed.

When we shot the pilot, I met Cory Monteith, Kevin McHale, Amber Riley, and Chris Colfer for the first time. I had worked on Broadway with Jenna Ushkowitz and Matt Morrison before. Matt had been a friend of mine for years,

← From left to right: Kristin Chenoweth and me accepting our platinum records for Glee ✳ Cory in one of the White House hallways—with a bunny, of course—when we sang for the president and his family on Easter ✳ Chris Colfer in the White House ✳ Ryan Murphy and me receiving our first Glee platinum record ✳ Cory in the White House.

and in fact we'd actually dated back in the day for a Broadway beat. But strangers or not, we were all babies and completely new to the big-time spotlight. Cory came from Canada and drove his Honda Civic all the way to Los Angeles. Chris Colfer was from Clovis, California, and had never worked professionally in his life. Kevin McHale and Amber Riley were two of the most talented people I had ever met but were also reasonably new to the television world. It was really only Jane Lynch who was known—she was the one getting the TV show its initial credibility.

We all clicked like we were brothers and sisters and were inseparable from the start. When we shot the pilot we knew that it was something special, but just because a show is something special doesn't mean it's necessarily going to get picked up and have a life on TV. I was living in New York at the time, so when shooting wrapped I headed home. Jenna was staying with me, and Chris came to visit New York for the first time. I got to show him Times Square and the *Wicked* theater. (Flash forward five years and we were in front of that same theater shooting *Glee*.) The three of us were hanging out at my house in New York when I got the e-mail from Ryan telling me that we got picked up for thirteen episodes. I printed that message out and still have it, because that's the moment when my life completely changed. And it changed quickly: We shot the pilot in October 2008, and we started filming the first thirteen episodes in January 2009, in a total bubble. Nobody knew who we were or what

Glee was, and so it was a very pure time for all of us. When the show finally aired in September 2009, everything changed overnight: The show was a sensation. We were nominated for awards (Chris won a Golden Globe; I was nominated for an Emmy and for a best-actress-in-a-comedy Golden Globe), we were on *Oprah,* we met the president, and we went around the world on live tours. There was merchandise, there were Christmas records, there was porn made in our honor. It was amazing. But it was hard, too.

Suddenly, we were becoming famous: Paparazzi became interested in my comings and goings, our pictures were in magazines, and people started to decide who I was. They decided, for one, that I was a diva—but not a diva in the way I had always wanted to be (a Broadway diva, the best thing ever!). The "high-maintenance diva" accusation was frustrating because I'm the farthest thing from that: I'm just a girl who knows who she is and what she wants, and I tend to speak my mind. What's disappointing is that there are so many people in this business who are not nice and who are difficult to work with but pretend like they're not. I guess at the end of the day I'd rather be misjudged than pretend to be someone I'm not and be publicly liked for being fake. That period definitely thickened my skin, as I learned quickly that I can't control other people's opinions. I really try to not let things like that get to me anymore. I thank my family and good friends for knowing who I really am and making that what matters most.

Thankfully, we're all pretty grounded kids who come from great families, which was essential for getting us through that first onslaught of interest and press. Without that sort of support, it could have been scary. I also credit Ryan for seeing us through, because as much as we were part of a huge machine that was propelling us forward, he cared about us. Before our first Golden Globes, he took all of the girls shopping and helped us pick out our dresses. And then he bought them for us, so that we could keep them with us for the rest of our lives.

I get asked a lot about the best moments from the beginning. When I look back, a few snapshots really stand out: Looking at my mom in the audience while I was onstage with Oprah; sitting in the box at the Super Bowl with my dad after singing "God Bless America"; peeing at the White House and stealing toilet paper that had the White House seal on it; standing onstage singing "Empire State of Mind" in New York City during our second concert tour. There are so many other amazing moments, but those are the ones I most remember.

The cast of *Glee* is amazing, and I can't say enough good things about them. While we don't hang out as much in our downtime now as we did on day one, when we were inseparable, our connection now is deeper. They are my family. Amber will text me out of the blue just to tell me that she loves me—so will Kevin McHale. And Chris Colfer is one of the loves of my life—I see us in forty years in some Broadway revival,

sipping martinis and reminiscing about the good old days. I've known Jenna since I was a kid (when we got to work together on *Spring Awakening*). And then there's Cory, who played such a large role in the show and also in my personal life.

Even though we're in our fifth season, and these past five years have been filled with the greatest ups, some difficult downs, and then, of course, terrible tragedy, I still love *Glee* as much today as I did at the beginning. It is a home for me, where I am surrounded by what has become an extended family—the cast and crew of *Glee* bring me the same comfort and joy as my own parents.

I try not to set limits for myself anymore, because the original limits that I set were proven completely wrong. Here I am now: I have the lead on a TV show, I have a L'Oréal campaign, and I've been on the cover of some of my favorite beauty magazines. So here's a big fat middle finger to the lady who told me to get my nose done.

Clockwise from top left: Dressed up as Gaga for our Lady Gaga episode ❖ trip to Disneyland with my mom, Jonathan Groff, and the _Glee_ kids ❖ Cory and me on the lawn of the White House ❖ the "Total Eclipse of the Heart" dance number, which was one of my favorites from _Glee_ ❖ dressed up as a cupcake, taking a hilarious photo with Amber ❖ Oprah and me ❖ Chris posing with Hillary at the White House ❖ Chord, Amber, Kevin, and me at the Golden Globes.

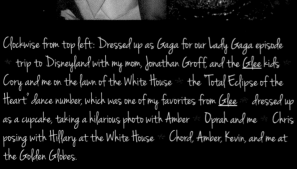

FAN QUESTIONS

Q: WHAT WAS THE FUNNIEST THING TO HAPPEN ON SET?

A: I had to do a scene where a very intense and determined Rachel rushes into the room and exclaims, "Listen, everybody, this is what happened." I didn't realize but my shirt had busted open. Luckily, I was wearing a bra, but still—nobody called cut! I was totally embarrassed.

Q: WHAT WAS THE FIRST _GLEE_ SCENE YOU EVER SHOT?

A: The very first scene we shot is a moment when Rachel is the in the women's bathroom, looking at herself in the mirror, and Santana and Quinn laugh at her. I remember being nervous at the time but thinking that the first day went well.

Q: WHAT WAS THE MOST DIFFICULT SONG TO SING?

A: "I Was Here" by Beyoncé, which ultimately didn't make it onto the show (it's on one of the albums). It was incredibly challenging. I also had a lot of trouble with "Take a Bow" by Rihanna in episode 2. It was the first time I'd ever tried to sing a pop song, since I'd spent my career singing classic rock and Broadway show tunes. Ryan was going to cut it and have me sing "I Don't Know How to Love Him"

from _Jesus Christ Superstar_ instead, but we made "Take a Bow" work because it was so perfect for the story.

Q: WHAT WAS THE HARDEST THING YOU EVER HAD TO DO ON SET?

A: In an episode called "Wheels," there's a scene where I had to put my face into a plate of fettuccine Alfredo. I had to pretend I'd been hit and fall into the tray. I know it's theoretically not hard, but it really was the most disgusting thing in the entire world.

Q: WHAT ARE YOUR FAVORITE EPISODES?

A: "Pilot"
"The Break Up"
"Showmance"
"Journey"
"New York"

Q: WHAT ARE YOUR FAVORITE MOMENTS?

A: When Rachel tells Finn, "You can kiss me if you want to."

When Rachel sings "Don't Rain on My Parade"

When Kurt sings "Being Alive"

When Kurt and Rachel are outside of Tiffany

The "At the Ballet" number with Sarah Jessica Parker

Q: WHAT ARE YOUR FAVORITE GLEE SONGS?

A: "Shake It Out"

"Anything Could Happen"

"Americano/Dance Again"

"Safety Dance"

"Empire State of Mind"

Q: WHAT WERE YOUR FAVORITE GUEST-STAR MOMENTS?

A: Singing "Maybe This Time" with Kristin Chenoweth

Dancing to *Chicago* with Gwyneth Paltrow

Anything and everything with Kate Hudson

Getting a makeover from Sarah Jessica Parker

Getting to pretend-date Jonathan Groff

Q: HOW DO YOU HANDLE THE PAPARAZZI?

A: The paparazzi exist in New York, but in a very understated way; in Los Angeles, they're a huge (and dangerous) part of the culture. I get far less paparazzi pressure than a lot of celebrities in this city, but I still find their attention confounding. I'm a very grounded person—my day-to-day activities just aren't that interesting. The fact that they want to capture me going into, and leaving, Whole Foods just sort of confuses me—and it makes me sad when they'll run red lights and endanger other people just to get that shot. I absolutely understand that it comes with the job, but I don't think that nearly causing accidents is worth it. Ultimately, I don't let the paparazzi ever stop me from carrying on with my life—they're not going to catch me doing anything scandalous, after all!

The other downside of the paparazzi, and being a public person, is that there are days when you really just don't want your photo taken. When that's the case, I lie low, cook at home, and stay out of the public eye. In my real life, I'm not like Rachel Berry, who could probably think of nothing she'd like more than showing off eighteen different rehearsed smiles and poses for the paps.

Clockwise from top left: Dressed up as football players with Jenna, which was one of my favorite scenes ever on _Glee_ ❖ ballerinas from "Total Eclipse of the Heart" ❖ Chris Colfer and me on set ❖ filming our Christmas episode ❖ Heather, Jenna, Cory, and me in London during our _Glee_ tour ❖ filming _Glee_ in New York with Chris during Season 4 ❖ everyone made fun of the dress I wore to the White House, but I really thought it was the most appropriate option ❖ Darren, Kevin, and me all danced out.

FINDING TIME TO TAKE CARE OF YOURSELF (SLEEP, ETC.)/DEALING WITH LONG HOURS

Even though it's calmed down considerably from the beginning, *Glee* is incredibly demanding to film: At the beginning, we were shooting twenty-two episodes and then going straight into a tour. There were moments when we all felt like we were about to break, but I think most of us came out the better for it. But while it's less grueling than it was five years ago, it's still pretty all-consuming. Because of that, I don't have much of a social life outside of the show. After work, I generally head straight home to get as much rest and sleep as possible, since self-care is my number one priority. While the rest of the cast can somehow find it within themselves to go out at night, I'm the show's old lady.

↑ Whenever we were doing a ridiculously long dance number on <u>Glee</u>, the hair and makeup team and I would commemorate the moment with a photo of me passed out on the floor. I have about 100 of these. This came from about hour ten of a particularly grueling number: we were doing "Time Warp" from <u>Rocky Horror Picture Show</u>.

A DAY IN THE LIFE OF *GLEE*

I think Lou, our costume designer, said it best: Shooting an episode of *Glee* is like jumping out of an airplane and needing to learn the choreography, learn your lines, learn your songs, and film everything before you crash on the ground. There are so many different components to stitching an episode together, it's shocking it all gets done.

DURING ANY GIVEN WEEK, ON THE DAYS WHEN YOU'RE NOT SHOOTING . . .

You have dance rehearsal with Brooke Lipton.

Then you have sessions with the very brilliant Adam and Alex Anders to record the songs.

Next, you do fittings with the wardrobe team and set your costumes.

You can't forget to learn your lines.

And then you shoot.

Our crew is the hardest-working crew in the entire business. Generally, they work all day and all night. There are times when we have a six a.m. call time and don't wrap until three a.m., working that entire time. Sometimes we have to do three musical numbers in a single day. I've been known to fall asleep on the floor many, many times.

Probably the hardest number to ever do physically was the one in the swimming pool. And the food fight was particularly unfun. And then there was the "Thriller" number, which we had to do at night. We began shooting at eight p.m. and didn't wrap until seven a.m. That was the first all-nighter I'd ever pulled. Ever! As you probably know by now, I'm not a party girl, and I've never watched the sun come up after staying up all night. After taping that particular episode, I called my dad and made him talk to me as I drove home from Long Beach—I was terrified I would fall asleep behind the wheel. Thankfully, he kept me company the whole ride home. I was so exhausted, that night definitely turned that episode into one of the most memorable for me of all five seasons.

> HIGH SCHOOL KIDS EVERYWHERE CAN SEE THEMSELVES IN THE CHARACTERS ON *GLEE*, AND PARENTS HAVE FOUND NEW AVENUES FOR CONVERSATION WITH THEIR CHILDREN. AND WE'VE ALL BEEN ENTERTAINED.

THE MYSTIQUE OF RYAN MURPHY

The privilege of meeting, knowing, and getting to work with the genius that is Ryan Murphy is one of the greatest things about being on *Glee*. I think I'm stealing this quote from Chris Colfer, who said it when he was accepting his Golden Globe, but Ryan Murphy is my fairy godmother. After all, the first time I met Ryan, we spent the whole night talking about Barbra Streisand. I remember thinking that we were very alike and that he understood me. He's equally as intense and focused.

I'm grateful to Ryan for everything, but we should all be grateful, actually, because Ryan created a TV show that changed so many people's lives and opened so many eyes and minds: High school kids everywhere can see themselves in the characters on *Glee*, and parents have found new avenues for conversation with their children. And we've all been entertained.

Really, Ryan is superhuman: Besides running three television shows, directing movies, and being a father and a husband, he still finds the time to call me every week to check in—and catch up on what's going on with the Real Housewives. When I first moved to Los Angeles, Ryan knew the adjustment was hard—that I missed my life in New York and was struggling a bit to find my place in L.A. I was single, I was trying to make new friends, and I was far from my family, so he always tried to look out for me. One night, we met up for dinner, and he had bought me a

necklace, a really cool and funky necklace from Marni. I could tell he was shy and embarrassed to give it to me, but the fact that he had gone to Barneys to find something for himself and had ended up getting a present for me instead struck me as one of the nicest, most thoughtful gestures ever. One weekend, he knew I would be sitting around doing nothing, and so he invited me and Jonathan Groff to his house in Laguna. I woke up early in the morning, and Ryan was already up, in a very chic robe. He was just himself, at his simplest. I sat at the kitchen counter, and he said, "Let me make you some breakfast," and proceeded to pour me a bowl of cereal and hand me the paper. There was something about that very low-key moment that I'll always remember the most—just to see Ryan Murphy not as the man who runs the world, but as the genuine, heart-as-big-as-the-moon guy who made me a bowl of breakfast.

Nothing would make me happier than to work solely with Ryan Murphy for the rest of my career.

> I wanted this chapter to be at the end of the book because it represents where I am in life right now. I still love *Glee* as much as I did day one and am so excited to start the sixth season. I really can't wait to see what the show has in store for Rachel Berry and what lessons she'll learn next.

UNTIL
NEXT
TIME

Putting *Brunette Ambition* together has been a profound and powerful experience for me: Not only have I revisited all the life experiences that have made me the person I am today, but I've also been able to distill everything I've learned onto the pages of what I think is a very useful book. I hope you find it useful, too!

I may live *Brunette Ambition* every day, but I still turn back to its pages constantly, whether it's for a refresher course on Mark Townsend's Coconut Oil Hair Masque or guidance on doing an at-home workout when Devon isn't by my side. These are my life coaches, and so I'm thrilled to be able to share them with you. I'm also thrilled to be able to share my larger philosophy on getting everything I need to do done—all while reaching for the stars and beyond.

Ultimately, this is just the beginning of the Brunette Ambition movement: As my world continues to grow, as I learn a few more tips and tricks, there will be more and more to share. Thank you for reading and thank you for being amazing fans—your support means the world to me. And I can't wait to meet you all along the way.

ACKNOWLEDGMENTS

FIRST AND FOREMOST, I'd love to thank all the gleeks out there whose endless support and love constantly motivate me and give me so much strength and joy.

Mom and Dad, I love you both so much. It was so fun getting to write this book and to let the world know what an amazing family I have and how incredible you both are.

Estee Stanley, thank you so much for all your help with this book. You're such a beautiful and strong woman. Thank you for bringing that beauty into this book. And for always being there for me.

A very big thank-you to Mark Townsend and Jenna Hipp for their contribution to this book. Thank you both so much for all your hard work over the years. And, of course, Melanie, you have been by my side since the moment I arrived in Los Angeles and have been there for me ever since. You are so talented. Thank you for being my friend and for always making me look beautiful.

Alissa Vradenburg, you really are a superwoman. Between helping me with this book and my album and everything else, you still manage to be such an amazing friend and confidante. I can't thank you enough for all you've done for me over the past few years. When I needed you most, you were there for me. And that meant more to me than you'll ever know.

Justin Coit, you're so incredibly talented. Thank you for taking such gorgeous photos for this book.

Devon Butler, since the day I met you, you have been such a rock for me. I think you're one of the most amazing women I know. You're an incredible friend and mother, and a sick trainer! Thank you for all your help with this book. And for rocking that pregnant belly! PS, Devon gave birth to a beautiful baby girl, Juliette.

To all my amazing girlfriends who have been there for me through so much, I don't know what I'd do without you guys. Especially Jennifer (aka Snacks). We've been through so much together this past year. You are totally my Charlotte.

Jonathan Groff, I love you. I couldn't have gotten through this past year without you. Thank you for always being there for me and for being my best friend.

Elise Loehnen, what can I say? There aren't enough thank-yous to truly express to you how grateful I am for your help with this book. But more than anything, I'm so grateful that this book brought us together. I'm so honored to have been able to work with you and to now call you a friend.

A huge thank-you to all the amazing people at Crown Archetype: Tina Constable, Mauro DiPreta, Suzanne O'Neill, Tammy Blake, Julie Cepler, Anna Thompson, Michael Nagin, Elizabeth Rendfleisch, and Jennifer K. Beal Davis. Thank you for believing in me and for making this dream come true.

To Jennifer Rudolph Walsh, Andy McNicol, Jason Weinberg, Shelby Weiser, Will Ward; my agents, Stephanie Ritz and Sharon Jackson at WME; and Robert Offer. I love you guys so much. A huge thank-you to my very hardworking business manager, Adam.

And finally, to Cory. I'm so happy to know that you got to read this book. Thank you for all your notes. I promise I made every single one. I love you.

PHOTOGRAPHY CREDITS